"In this tight, engaging book, Ryan Holiday shines a bright, powerful light on the path to living and leading well. By showing us how to turn failure, obstacles, and plain old everyday frustration to our advantage, he offers up a host of easy-to-use tactics that each of us can put to work to follow our dreams. Read it , learn from it, and get cracking!"

—NANCY F. KOEHN, historian and leadership expert, Harvard Business School

"My life has been beset with obstacles. It takes practice (and pain) to surmount them and achieve success. Ryan's book is a how-to guide for just that."   —JAMES ALTUCHER, investor and author of *Choose Yourself*

"If there's such a thing as a cargo-pocket handbook for Jedi knights, this is it. Ryan Holiday's *The Obstacle is the Way* decants in concentrated form the timeless techniques for self-mastery as employed to world-conquering effect by philosophers and men of action from Alexander the Great to Marcus Aurelius to Steve Jobs. Follow these precepts and you will revolutionize your life. As Mr. Holiday writes, 'It's simple, it's just not easy.' Read this book!"   —STEVEN PRESSFIELD, author of *The War of Art* and *Gates of Fire*

PRAISE FOR *THE OBSTACLE IS THE WAY*

"A book for the bedside of every future—and curr
leader in the world."   —ROBERT GRE
                  author of *The 48 Laws of Power* and *M*

"Ryan brings philosophy out from the classroom and th
it back where it belongs, in our daily lives, helping an
approaching any problem address it with equanimity
poise. A kind of user's manual for life, you will turn
time and time again and learn to tear through any obst
and resolve any conflict. An absolute must-read."
                    —JIMMY SONI, managing edit
           The Huffington Post, author of *Rome's Last Ci*

"First came Marcus Aurelius, then Frederick the Great
and now there's you. This surprising book shows you hov
craft a life of wonder by embracing obstacles and challeng
                —CHRIS GUILLEBEAU, author of *The $100 Star*

THE
OBSTACLE
IS THE
WAY

THE
OBSTACLE
IS THE
WAY

THE TIMELESS ART OF
TURING TRIALS INTO TRIUMPH

Ryan Holiday

PORTFOLIO / PENGUIN

PORTFOLIO / PENGUIN

Published by the Penguin Group
Penguin Group (USA) LLC
375 Hudson Street
New York, New York 10014

USA | Canada | UK | Ireland | Australia | New Zealand | India | South
Africa | China
penguin.com
A Penguin Random House Company

First published by Portfolio / Penguin, a member of Penguin Group
(USA) LLC, 2014

LIBRARY OF CONGRESS CATALOGING-IN-PUBLICATION DATA
Holiday, Ryan.
The obstacle is the way : the timeless art of turning trials into triumph
/ Ryan Holiday.
pages cm
Includes bibliographical references.
ISBN 978-1-59184-635-2
1. Motivation (Psychology) 2. Self-realization. I. Title.
BF503.H65 2014
158—dc23

                                    2013039949

Printed in the United States of America
10 9 8 7 6 5 4 3 2 1

Set in ITC New Baskerville Std
Designed by E. J. Strongin, Neuwirth Associates, Inc.

CONTENTS

PART II: ACTION

PART III: WILL

PREFACE

In the year 170, at night in his tent on the front lines of the war in Germania, Marcus Aurelius, the emperor of the Roman Empire, sat down to write. Or perhaps it was before dawn at the palace in Rome. Or he stole a few seconds to himself during the games, ignoring the carnage on the floor of the Colosseum below. The exact location is not important. What matters is that this man, known today as the last of the Five Good Emperors, sat down to write.

Not to an audience or for publication but to himself, *for* himself. And what he wrote is undoubtedly one of history's most effective formulas for overcoming every negative situation we may encounter in life. A formula for thriving not just in spite of whatever happens but *because of it.*

At that moment, he wrote only a paragraph. Only a little of it was original. Almost every thought could, in some form or another, be found in the writings of his mentors and idols. But in a scant eighty-five words Marcus Aurelius so clearly defined and articulated a timeless idea that he eclipses the great names of those who came before him: Chrysippus, Zeno, Cleanthes, Ariston, Apollonius, Junius

Rusticus, Epictetus, Seneca, Musonius Rufus.

It is more than enough for us.

Our actions may be impeded . . . but there can be no impeding our intentions or dispositions. Because we can accommodate and adapt. The mind adapts and converts to its own purposes the obstacle to our acting.

And then he concluded with powerful words destined for maxim.

The impediment to action advances action.
What stands in the way becomes the way.

In Marcus's words is the secret to an art known as *turning obstacles upside down*. To act with "a reverse clause," so there is always a way out or another route to get to where you need to go. So that setbacks or problems are always expected and never permanent. Making certain that what impedes us can empower us.

Coming from this particular man, these were not idle words. In his own reign of some nineteen years, he would experience nearly constant war, a horrific plague, possible infidelity, an attempt at the throne by one of his closest allies, repeated and arduous travel across the empire—from Asia Minor to Syria, Egypt, Greece, and Austria—a rapidly depleting treasury, an incompetent and greedy stepbrother as co-emperor, and on and on and on.

And from what we know, he truly saw each and every one of these obstacles as an opportunity to practice some virtue: patience, courage, humility, resourcefulness, reason, justice, and creativity. The power he held never seemed to go to his head—neither did the stress or burden. He rarely rose to excess or anger, and never to hatred or bitterness. As Matthew Arnold, the essayist, remarked in 1863, in Marcus we find a man who held the highest and most powerful station in the world—and the universal verdict of the people around him was that he proved himself worthy of it.

It turns out that the wisdom of that short passage from Marcus Aurelius can be found in others as well, men and women who followed it like he did. In fact, it is a remarkable constant down through the ages.

One can trace the thread from those days in the decline and fall of the Roman Empire to the creative outpouring of the Renaissance to the breakthroughs of the Enlightenment. It's seen starkly in the pioneer spirit of the American West, the perseverance of the Union cause during the Civil War, and in the bustle of the Industrial Revolution. It appeared again in the bravery of the leaders of the civil rights movement and stood tall in the prison camps of Vietnam. And today it surges in the DNA of the entrepreneurs of Silicon Valley.

This philosophic approach is the driving force of self-made men and the succor to those in positions with great responsibility or great trouble. On the battlefield or in the boardroom, across oceans and many centuries, members of every group, gender, class, cause, and business have had to confront obstacles and struggle to overcome them—learning to turn those obstacles upside down.

That struggle is the one constant in all of their lives. Knowingly or not, each individual was a part of an ancient tradition, employing it to navigate the timeless terrain of opportunities and difficulties, trial and triumph.

We are the rightful heirs to this tradition. It's our birthright. Whatever we face, we have a choice: Will we be blocked by obstacles, or will we advance through and over them?

We might not be emperors, but the world is still constantly testing us. It asks: Are you worthy? Can you get past the things that inevitably fall in your way? Will you stand up and show us what you're made of?

Plenty of people have answered this question in the affirmative. And a rarer breed still has shown that they not only have what it takes, but they thrive and rally at every such challenge. That the challenge makes them better than if they'd never faced the adversity at all.

Now it's your turn to see if you're one of them, if you'll join their company.

This book will show you the way.

THE
OBSTACLE
IS THE
WAY

INTRODUCTION

This thing in front of you. This issue. This obstacle—this frustrating, unfortunate, problematic, unexpected problem preventing you from doing what you want to do. That thing you dread or secretly hope will never happen. What if it wasn't so bad?

What if embedded inside it or inherent in it were certain benefits—benefits only for you? What would you do? What do you think most people would do?

Probably what they've always done, and what you are doing right now: nothing.

Let's be honest: Most of us are paralyzed. Whatever our individual goals, most of us sit frozen before the many obstacles that lie ahead of us.

We wish it weren't true, but it is.

What blocks us is clear. Systemic: decaying institutions, rising unemployment, skyrocketing costs of education, and technological disruption. Individual: too short, too old, too scared, too poor, too stressed, no access, no backers, no confidence. How skilled we are at cataloging what holds us back!

Every obstacle is unique to each of us. But the responses they elicit are the same: Fear. Frustration. Confusion. Helplessness. Depression. Anger.

THE OBSTACLE IS THE WAY

You know what you want to do but it feels like some invisible enemy has you boxed in, holding you down with pillows. You try to get somewhere, but something invariably blocks the path, following and thwarting each move you make. You have just enough freedom to feel like you can move; just enough to feel like it's your fault when you can't seem to follow through or build momentum.

We're dissatisfied with our jobs, our relationships, our place in the world. We're trying to get somewhere, but something stands in the way.

So we do nothing.

We blame our bosses, the economy, our politicians, other people, or we write ourselves off as failures or our goals as impossible. When really only one thing is at fault: our attitude and approach.

There have been countless lessons (and books) about achieving success, but no one ever taught us how to overcome failure, how to think about obstacles, how to treat and triumph over them, and so we are stuck. Beset on all sides, many of us are disoriented, reactive, and torn. We have no idea what to do.

On the other hand, not everyone is paralyzed. We watch in awe as some seem to turn those very obstacles, which stymie us, into launching pads for themselves. How do they do that? What's the secret?

Even more perplexing, earlier generations faced worse problems with fewer safety nets and fewer tools. They dealt with the same obstacles we have today *plus* the ones they worked so hard to try to eliminate for their children and others. And yet . . . we're still stuck.

What do these figures have that we lack? What are we missing? It's simple: a method and a framework for understanding, appreciating, and acting upon the obstacles life throws at us.

John D. Rockefeller had it—for him it was cool headedness and self-discipline. Demosthenes, the great Athenian orator, had it—for him it was a relentless drive to improve himself through action and practice. Abraham Lincoln had it—for him it was humility, endurance, and compassionate will.

There are other names you'll see again and again in this book: Ulysses S. Grant. Thomas Edison. Margaret Thatcher. Samuel Zemurray. Amelia Earhart. Erwin Rommel. Dwight D. Eisenhower. Richard Wright. Jack Johnson. Theodore Roosevelt. Steve Jobs. James Stockdale. Laura Ingalls Wilder. Barack Obama.

Some of these men and women faced unimaginable horrors, from imprisonment to debilitating illnesses, in addition to day-to-day frustrations that were no different from ours. They dealt with the same rivalries, political headwinds, drama, resistance, conservatism, breakups, stresses, and economic calamities. Or worse.

Subjected to those pressures, these individuals were transformed. They were transformed along the lines that Andy Grove, former CEO of Intel, outlined when he described what happens to businesses in tumultuous times: "Bad companies are destroyed by crisis. Good companies survive them. Great companies are improved by them."

Great individuals, like great companies, find a way to transform weakness into strength. It's a rather amazing and even touching feat. They took what should have held them back—what in fact might be holding you back right this very second—and used it to move forward.

As it turns out, this is one thing all great men and women

of history have in common. Like oxygen to a fire, obstacles became fuel for the blaze that was their ambition. Nothing could stop them, they were (and continue to be) impossible to discourage or contain. Every impediment only served to make the inferno within them burn with greater ferocity.

These were people who flipped their obstacles upside down. Who lived the words of Marcus Aurelius and followed a group which Cicero called the only "real philosophers"— the ancient Stoics—even if they'd never read them.* They had the ability to see obstacles for what they were, the ingenuity to tackle them, and the will to endure a world mostly beyond their comprehension and control.

Let's be honest. Most of the time we don't find ourselves in horrible situations we must simply endure. Rather, we face some minor disadvantage or get stuck with some less-than-favorable conditions. Or we're trying to do something really hard and find ourselves outmatched, overstretched, or out of ideas. Well, the same logic applies. Turn it around. Find some benefit. Use it as fuel.

It's simple. Simple but, of course, not easy.

This is not a book of gushing, hazy optimism. This is not a book that tells you to deny when stuff sucks or to turn the other cheek when you've been completely screwed over. There will be no folksy sayings or cute but utterly ineffectual proverbs.

---

* I think Stoicism is a deeply fascinating and critically important philosophy. But I also understand that you live in the real world, right now, and you don't have time for a history lecture. What you want are real strategies to help you with your problems, so that's what this book is going to be. If you'd like some additional resources and reading recommendations on Stoicism, I've provided them in the reading list at the back of this book.

This is also not an academic study or history of Stoicism. There is plenty written about Stoicism out there, much of it by some of the wisest and greatest thinkers who ever lived. There is no need to rewrite what they have written—go read the originals. No philosophic writing is more accessible. It feels like it was written last year, not last millennium.

But I have done my best to collect, understand, and now publish their lessons and tricks. Ancient philosophy never cared much for authorship or originality—all writers did their best to translate and explain the wisdom of the greats as it has been passed down in books, diaries, songs, poems, and stories. All of these, refined in the crucible of human experience over thousands of years.

This book will share with you their collective wisdom in order to help you accomplish the very specific and increasingly urgent goal we all share: overcoming obstacles. Mental obstacles. Physical obstacles. Emotional obstacles. Perceived obstacles.

We face them every day and our society is collectively paralyzed by this. If all this book does is make facing and dismantling such stumbling blocks a little easier, it will be enough. But my aim is higher. I want to show you the way to turn every obstacle into an *advantage*.

So this will be a book of ruthless pragmatism and stories from history that illustrate the arts of relentless persistence and indefatigable ingenuity. It teaches you how to get unstuck, unfucked, and unleashed. How to turn the many negative situations we encounter in our lives into positive ones—or at least to snatch whatever benefit we can from them. To steal good fortune from misfortune.

It's not just: *How can I think* this is not so bad? No, it is how to will yourself to see that this must be good—an opportunity to gain a new foothold, move forward, or go in a better direction. Not "be positive" but learn to be ceaselessly creative and opportunistic.

Not: *This is not so bad.*

But: *I can make this good.*

Because it can be done. In fact, it has and *is* being done. Every day. That's the power we will unlock in this book.

The Obstacles That Lie Before Us

There is an old Zen story about a king whose people had grown soft and entitled. Dissatisfied with this state of affairs, he hoped to teach them a lesson. His plan was simple: He would place a large boulder in the middle of the main road, completely blocking entry into the city. He would then hide nearby and observe their reactions.

How would they respond? Would they band together to remove it? Or would they get discouraged, quit, and return home?

With growing disappointment, the king watched as subject after subject came to this impediment and turned away. Or, at best, tried halfheartedly before giving up. Many openly complained or cursed the king or fortune or bemoaned the inconvenience, but none managed to do anything about it.

After several days, a lone peasant came along on his way into town. He did not turn away. Instead he strained and strained, trying to push it out of the way. Then an idea came to him: He scrambled into the nearby woods to find something he could use for leverage. Finally, he returned with a large branch he had crafted into a lever and deployed it to dislodge the massive rock from the road.

Beneath the rock were a purse of gold coins and a note from the king, which said:

"The obstacle in the path becomes the path. Never forget, within every obstacle is an opportunity to improve our condition."

What holds you back?

The Physical? Size. Race. Distance. Disability. Money.

The Mental? Fear. Uncertainty. Inexperience. Prejudice.

Perhaps people don't take you seriously. Or you think you're too old. Or you lack support or enough resources. Maybe laws or regulations restrict your options. Or your obligations do. Or false goals and self-doubt.

Whatever it is, here you are. Here we all are.

And . . .

These are obstacles. I get it. No one is denying that.

But run down the list of those who came before you. Athletes who were too small. Pilots whose eyesight wasn't good enough. Dreamers ahead of their time. Members of this race or that. Dropouts and dyslexics. Bastards, immigrants, nouveaux riches, sticklers, believers, and dreamers. Or those who came from nothing or worse, from places where their very existence was threatened on a daily basis. What happened to them?

Well, far too many gave up. But a few didn't. They took "twice as good" as a challenge. They practiced harder. Looked for shortcuts and weak spots. Discerned allies among strange faces. Got kicked around a bit. *Everything* was an obstacle they had to flip.

And so?

Within those obstacles was an opportunity. They seized it. They did something special because of it. We can learn from them.

Whether we're having trouble getting a job, fighting against discrimination, running low on funds, stuck in a bad relationship, locking horns with some aggressive opponent, have an employee or student we just can't seem to reach, or are in the middle of a creative block, we need to know that there is a way. When we meet with adversity, we can turn it to advantage, based on their example.

All great victories, be they in politics, business, art, or seduction, involved resolving vexing problems with a potent cocktail of creativity, focus, and daring. When you have a goal, obstacles are actually teaching you how to get where you want to go—carving you a path. "The Things which hurt," Benjamin Franklin wrote, *"instruct."*

Today, most of our obstacles are internal, not external. Since World War II we have lived in some of the most prosperous times in history. There are fewer armies to face, fewer fatal diseases and far more safety nets. But the world still rarely does exactly what we want.

Instead of opposing enemies, we have internal tension. We have professional frustration. We have unmet expectations. We have learned helplessness. And we still have the same overwhelming emotions humans have always had: grief, pain, loss.

Many of our problems come from having too much: rapid technological disruption, junk food, traditions that tell us the way we're supposed to live our lives. We're soft, entitled, and scared of conflict. Great times are great softeners.

Abundance can be its own obstacle, as many people can attest.

Our generation needs an approach for overcoming obstacles and thriving amid chaos more than ever. One that will help turn our problems on their heads, using them as canvases on which to paint master works. This flexible approach is fit for an entrepreneur or an artist, a conqueror or a coach, whether you're a struggling writer or a sage or a hardworking soccer mom.

The Way Through Them

Objective judgment, now at this very moment.
Unselfish action, now at this very moment.
Willing acceptance—now at this very moment—of all external events.
That's all you need.

—MARCUS AURELIUS

Overcoming obstacles is a discipline of three critical steps.

It begins with how we look at our specific problems, our attitude or approach; then the energy and creativity with which we actively break them down and turn them into opportunities; finally, the cultivation and maintenance of an inner will that allows us to handle defeat and difficulty.

It's three interdependent, interconnected, and fluidly contingent disciplines: *Perception*, *Action*, and the *Will*.

It's a simple process (but again, never easy).

We will trace the use of this process by its practitioners throughout history, business, and literature. As we look at specific examples of each step from every angle, we'll learn to inculcate this attitude and capture its ingenuity—and by doing so discover how to create new openings wherever a door is shut.

From the stories of the practitioners we'll learn how to handle common obstacles—whether we're locked out or hemmed in, the kind of obstacles that have impeded people for all time—and how to apply their general approach to our lives. Because obstacles are not only to be expected but embraced.

Embraced?

Yes, because these obstacles are actually opportunities to test ourselves, to try new things, and, ultimately, to triumph.

The Obstacle Is the Way.

PART I

Perception

WHAT IS PERCEPTION? It's how we see and understand what occurs around us—and what we decide those events will mean. Our perceptions can be a source of strength or of great weakness. If we are emotional, subjective and short-sighted, we only add to our troubles. To prevent becoming overwhelmed by the world around us, we must, as the ancients practiced, learn how to limit our passions and their control over our lives. It takes skill and discipline to bat away the pests of bad perceptions, to separate reliable signals from deceptive ones, to filter out prejudice, expectation, and fear. But it's worth it, for what's left is *truth*. While others are excited or afraid, we will remain calm and imperturbable. We will see things simply and straightforwardly, as they truly are—neither good nor bad. This will be an incredible advantage for us in the fight against obstacles.

THE DISCIPLINE OF PERCEPTION

B efore he was an oilman, John D. Rockefeller was a bookkeeper and aspiring investor—a small-time financier in Cleveland, Ohio. The son of an alcoholic criminal who'd abandoned his family, the young Rockefeller took his first job in 1855 at the age of sixteen (a day he celebrated as "Job Day" for the rest of his life). All was well enough at fifty cents a day.

Then the panic struck. Specifically, the Panic of 1857, a massive national financial crisis that originated in Ohio and hit Cleveland particularly hard. As businesses failed and the price of grain plummeted across the country, westward expansion quickly came to a halt. The result was a crippling depression that lasted for several years.

Rockefeller could have gotten scared. Here was the greatest market depression in history and it hit him just as he was finally getting the hang of things. He could have pulled out and run like his father. He could have quit finance altogether for a different career with less risk. But even as a young man, Rockefeller had sangfroid: unflappable coolness under pressure. He could keep his head while he was losing his shirt. Better yet, he kept his head while everyone else lost theirs.

And so instead of bemoaning this economic upheaval, Rockefeller eagerly observed the momentous events. Almost perversely, he chose to look at it all as an opportunity to learn, a baptism in the market. He quietly saved his money and watched what others did wrong. He saw the weaknesses in the economy that many took for granted and how this left them all unprepared for change or shocks.

He internalized an important lesson that would stay with him forever: The market was inherently unpredictable and often vicious—only the rational and disciplined mind could hope to profit from it. Speculation led to disaster, he realized, and he needed to always ignore the "mad crowd" and its inclinations.

Rockefeller immediately put those insights to use. At twenty-five, a group of investors offered to invest approximately $500,000 at his direction if he could find the right oil wells in which to deploy the money. Grateful for the opportunity, Rockefeller set out to tour the nearby oil fields. A few days later, he shocked his backers by returning to Cleveland empty-handed, not having spent or invested a dollar of the funds. The opportunity didn't feel right to him at the time, no matter how excited the rest of the market was—so he refunded the money and stayed away from drilling.

It was this intense self-discipline and objectivity that allowed Rockefeller to seize advantage from obstacle after obstacle in his life, during the Civil War, and the panics of 1873, 1907, and 1929. As he once put it: He was inclined to see the opportunity in every disaster. To that we could add: He had the strength to resist temptation or excitement, no matter how seductive, no matter the situation.

Within twenty years of that first crisis, Rockefeller would alone control 90 percent of the oil market. His greedy competitors had perished. His nervous colleagues had sold their shares and left the business. His weak-hearted doubters had missed out.

For the rest of his life, the greater the chaos, the calmer Rockefeller would become, particularly when others around him were either panicked or mad with greed. He would make much of his fortune during these market fluctuations—because he could see while others could not. This insight lives on today in Warren Buffet's famous adage to "be fearful when others are greedy and greedy when others are fearful." Rockefeller, like all great investors, could resist impulse in favor of cold, hard common sense.

One critic, in awe of Rockefeller's empire, described the Standard Oil trust as a "mythical protean creature" capable of metamorphosing with every attempt by the competitors or the government to dismantle it. They meant it as a criticism, but it was actually a function of Rockefeller's personality: resilient, adaptable, calm, brilliant. He could not be rattled—not by economic crisis, not by a glittery mirage of false opportunities, not by aggressive, bullying enemies, not even by federal prosecutors (for whom he was a notoriously difficult witness to cross-examine, never rising to take the bait or defend himself or get upset).

Was he born this way? No. This was learned behavior. And Rockefeller got this lesson in discipline somewhere. It began in that crisis of 1857 in what he called "the school of adversity and stress."

"Oh, how blessed young men are who have to struggle for a foundation and beginning in life," he once said. "I shall never cease to be grateful for the three and half years of apprenticeship and the difficulties to be overcome, all along the way."

Of course, many people experienced the same perilous times as Rockefeller—they all attended the same school of bad times. But few reacted as he did. Not many had trained themselves to see opportunity inside this obstacle, that what befell them was not unsalvageable misfortune but the gift of education—a chance to *learn* from a rare moment in economic history.

You will come across obstacles in life—fair and unfair. And you will discover, time and time again, that what matters most is not what these obstacles are but how we see them, how we react to them, and whether we keep our composure. You will learn that this reaction determines how successful we will be in overcoming—or possibly thriving because of—them.

Where one person sees a crisis, another can see opportunity. Where one is blinded by success, another sees reality with ruthless objectivity. Where one loses control of emotions, another can remain calm. Desperation, despair, fear, powerlessness—these reactions are functions of our perceptions. You must realize: Nothing *makes* us feel this way; we *choose* to give in to such feelings. Or, like Rockefeller, choose *not* to.

And it is precisely at this divergence—between how Rockefeller perceived his environment and how the rest of the world typically does—that his nearly incomprehensible success was born. His careful, cautious self-confidence was an incredible form of power. To perceive what others see as negative, as something to be approached rationally, clearly, and, most important, as an opportunity—not as something to fear or bemoan.

Rockefeller is more than just an analogy.

We live in our own Gilded Age. In less than a decade, we've experienced two major economic bubbles, entire industries are crumbling, lives have been disrupted. What feels like unfairness abounds. Financial downturns, civil unrest, adversity. People are afraid and discouraged, angry and upset and gathered in Zuccotti Park or in communities online. As they should be, right?

Not necessarily.

Outward appearances are deceptive. What's within them, beneath them, is what matters.

We can learn to perceive things differently, to cut through the illusions that others believe or fear. We can stop seeing the "problems" in front of us as problems. We can learn to focus on what things really are.

Too often we react emotionally, get despondent, and lose our perspective. All that does is turn bad things into really bad things. Unhelpful perceptions can invade our minds—that sacred place of reason, action and will—and throw off our compass.

Our brains evolved for an environment very different from the one we currently inhabit. As a result, we carry all kinds of biological baggage. Humans are still primed to detect threats and dangers that no longer exist—think of the cold sweat when you're stressed about money, or the fight-or-flight response that kicks in when your boss yells at you. Our safety is not truly at risk here—there is little danger that we will starve or that violence will break out—though it certainly feels that way sometimes.

We have a choice about how we respond to this situation (or any situation, for that matter). We can be blindly led by these primal feelings or we can understand them and learn to filter them. Discipline in perception lets you clearly see the advantage and the proper course of action in every situation—without the pestilence of panic or fear.

Rockefeller understood this well and threw off the fetters of bad, destructive perceptions. He honed the ability to control and channel and understand these signals. It was like a superpower; because most people can't access this part of themselves, they are slaves to impulses and instincts they have never questioned.

We can see disaster rationally. Or rather, like Rockefeller, we can see *opportunity* in every disaster, and transform that negative situation into an education, a skill set, or a fortune. Seen properly, everything that happens—be it an economic crash or a personal tragedy—is a chance to move forward. Even if it is on a bearing that we did not anticipate.

There are a few things to keep in mind when faced with a seemingly insurmountable obstacle. We must try:

- To be objective
- To control emotions and keep an even keel
- To choose to see the good in a situation
- To steady our nerves
- To ignore what disturbs or limits others
- To place things in perspective
- To revert to the present moment
- To focus on what can be controlled

This is how you see the opportunity within the obstacle. It does not happen on its own. It is a process—one that results from self-discipline and logic.

And that logic is available to you. You just need to deploy it.

RECOGNIZE YOUR POWER

Choose not to be harmed—and you won't feel harmed.
Don't feel harmed—and you haven't been.

—MARCUS AURELIUS

Rubin "Hurricane" Carter, a top contender for the middleweight title, at the height of his boxing career in the mid-1960s, was wrongly accused of a horrific crime he did not commit: triple homicide. He went on trial, and a biased, bogus verdict followed: three life sentences.

It was a dizzying fall from the heights of success and fame. Carter reported to prison in an expensive, tailored suit, wearing a $5,000 diamond ring and a gold watch. And so, waiting in line to be entered into the general inmate population, he asked to speak to someone in charge.

Looking the warden in the eye, Carter proceeded to inform him and the guards that he was not giving up the last thing he controlled: himself. In his remarkable declaration, he told them, in so many words, "I know you had nothing to do with the injustice that brought me to this jail, so I'm willing to stay here until I get out. But I will not, under any circumstances, be treated like a prisoner—because I am not and never will be *powerless*."

Instead of breaking down—as many would have done in such a bleak situation—Carter declined to surrender the freedoms that were innately his: his attitude, his beliefs, his choices. Whether they threw him in prison or threw him in solitary confinement for weeks on end, Carter maintained that he still had choices, choices that could not be taken from him even though his physical freedom had been.

Was he angry about what happened? Of course. He was furious. But understanding that anger was not constructive, he refused to rage. He refused to break or grovel or despair. He would not wear a uniform, eat prison food, accept visitors, attend parole hearings, or work in the commissary to reduce his sentence. And he wouldn't be touched. No one could lay a hand on him, unless they wanted a fight.

All of this had a purpose: Every second of his energy was to be spent on his legal case. Every waking minute was spent reading—law books, philosophy, history. They hadn't ruined his life—they'd just put him somewhere he didn't deserve to be and he did not intend to stay there. He would learn and read and make the most of the time he had on his hands. He would leave prison not only a free and innocent man, but a better and improved one.

It took nineteen years and two trials to overturn that verdict, but when Carter walked out of prison, he simply resumed his life. No civil suit to recover damages, Carter did not even request an apology from the court. Because to him, that would imply that they'd taken something of his that Carter felt he was owed. That had never been his view, even in the dark depths of solitary confinement. He had made his choice: This can't harm me—I might not have wanted it to happen, but I decide how it will affect me. *No one else has the right.*

We decide what we will make of each and every situation. We decide whether we'll break or whether we'll resist. We decide whether we'll assent or reject. No one can force us to give up or to believe something that is untrue (such as, that a situation is absolutely hopeless or impossible to improve). Our perceptions are the thing that we're in complete control of.

They can throw us in jail, label us, deprive us of our possessions, but they'll never control our thoughts, our beliefs, our *reactions*.

Which is to say, we are never completely powerless.

Even in prison, deprived of nearly everything, some freedoms remain. Your mind remains your own (if you're lucky, you have books) and you have time—lots of time. Carter did not have much power, but he understood that that was not the same thing as being *powerless*. Many great figures, from Nelson Mandela to Malcolm X, have come to understand this fundamental distinction. It's how they turned prison into the workshop where they transformed themselves and the schoolhouse where they began to transform others.

If an unjust prison sentence can be not only salvaged but transformative and beneficial, then for our purposes, nothing we'll experience is likely without potential benefit. In fact, if we have our wits fully about us, we can step back and remember that situations, by themselves, cannot be good or bad. This is something—a judgment—that we, as human beings, bring to them with our perceptions.

To one person a situation may be negative. To another, that same situation may be positive.

"Nothing either good or bad, but thinking makes it so," as Shakespeare put it.

Laura Ingalls Wilder, author of the classic series *Little House*, lived that idea, facing some of the toughest and unwelcoming elements on the planet: harsh and unyielding soil, Indian territory, Kansas prairies, and the humid backwoods of Florida. Not afraid, not jaded—because she saw it all as an adventure. Everywhere was a chance to do something new, to persevere with cheery pioneer spirit whatever fate befell her and her husband.

That isn't to say she saw the world through delusional rose-colored glasses. Instead, she simply chose to see each situation for what it could be—accompanied by hard work and a little upbeat spirit. Others make the opposite choice. As for us, we face things that are not nearly as intimidating, and then we promptly decide we're screwed.

This is how obstacles become obstacles.

In other words, through our perception of events, we are complicit in the creation—as well as the destruction—of every one of our obstacles.

There is no good or bad without us, there is only perception. There is the event itself and the story we tell ourselves about what it means.

That's a thought that changes everything, doesn't it?

An employee in your company makes a careless mistake that costs you business. This can be exactly what you spend so much time and effort trying to avoid. *Or,* with a shift in perception, it can be exactly what you were looking for—the chance to pierce through defenses and teach a lesson that can be learned only by experience. A *mistake* becomes *training.*

Again, the event is the same: Someone messed up. But the evaluation and the outcome are different. With one approach you took advantage; with the other you succumbed to anger or fear.

Just because your mind tells you that something is awful or evil or unplanned or otherwise negative doesn't mean you have to agree. Just because other people say that something is hopeless or crazy or broken to pieces doesn't mean it is. We decide what story to tell ourselves. Or whether we will tell one at all.

Welcome to the power of perception. Applicable in each and every situation, impossible to obstruct. It can only be *relinquished*.

And that is your decision.

STEADY YOUR NERVES

What such a man needs is not courage but nerve control, cool headedness. This he can get only by practice.

—THEODORE ROOSEVELT

Ulysses S. Grant once sat for a photo shoot with the famous Civil War photographer, Mathew Brady. The studio was too dark, so Brady sent an assistant up to the roof to uncover a skylight. The assistant slipped and shattered the window. With horror, the spectators watched as shards of glass two inches long fell from the ceiling like daggers, crashing around Grant—each one of them plenty lethal.

As the last pieces hit the ground, Brady looked over and saw that Grant hadn't moved. He was unhurt. Grant glanced up at the hole in the ceiling, then back at the camera as though nothing had happened at all.

During the Overland Campaign, Grant was surveying the scene through field glasses when an enemy shell exploded, killing the horse immediately next to him. Grant's eyes stayed fixed on the front, never leaving the glasses. There's another story about Grant at City Point, Union headquarters, near Richmond. Troops were unloading a steamboat and it suddenly exploded. Everyone hit the dirt except

Grant, who was seen running *toward* the scene of the explosion as debris and shells and even bodies rained down.

That's a man who has steadied himself properly. That's a man who has a job to do and would bear anything to get it done. That's nerve.

But back in our lives . . .

We are a pile of raw nerves.

Competitors surround our business. Unexpected problems suddenly rear their heads. Our best worker suddenly quits. The computer system can't handle the load we're putting on it. We're out of our comfort zone. The boss is making us do all the work. Everything is falling and crashing down around us, exactly when we feel like we can't handle any more.

Do we stare it down? Ignore it? Blink once or twice and redouble our concentration? Or do we get shaken up? Do we try to medicate these "bad" feelings away?

And that's just the stuff that happens unintentionally. Don't forget, there are always people out there looking to get you. They want to intimidate you. Rattle you. Pressure you into making a decision before you've gotten all the facts. They want you thinking and acting on their terms, not yours.

So the question is, are you going to let them?

When we aim high, pressure and stress obligingly come along for the ride. Stuff is going to happen that catches us off guard, threatens or scares us. Surprises (unpleasant ones, mostly) are almost guaranteed. The risk of being overwhelmed is always there.

In these situations, talent is not the most sought-after characteristic. Grace and poise are, because these two attributes precede the opportunity to deploy any other skill. We must possess, as Voltaire once explained about the secret to the great military success of the first Duke of Marlborough, that "tranquil courage in the midst of tumult and serenity of soul in danger, which the English call a cool head."

Regardless of how much actual danger we're in, stress puts us at the potential whim of our baser—fearful—instinctual reactions.

Don't think for a second that grace and poise and serenity are the soft attributes of some aristocrat. Ultimately, nerve is a matter of defiance and control.

Like: *I refuse to acknowledge that. I don't agree to be intimidated. I resist the temptation to declare this a failure.*

But nerve is also a matter of acceptance: *Well, I guess it's on me then. I don't have the luxury of being shaken up about this or replaying close calls in my head. I'm too busy and too many people are counting on me.*

Defiance and acceptance come together well in the following principle: There is always a countermove, always an escape or a way through, so there is no reason to get worked up. No one said it would be easy and, of course, the stakes are high, but the path is there for those ready to take it.

This is what we've got to do. And we know that it's going to be tough, maybe even scary.

But we're ready for that. We're collected and serious and aren't going to be frightened off.

This means preparing for the realities of our situation, steadying our nerves so we can throw our best at it. Steeling ourselves. Shaking off the bad stuff as it happens and soldiering on—staring straight ahead as though nothing has happened.

Because, as you now realize, it's true. If your nerve holds, then nothing really did "happen"—our perception made sure it was nothing of consequence.

CONTROL YOUR EMOTIONS

Would you have a great empire? Rule over yourself.

—PUBLIUS SYRUS

When America raced to send the first men into space, they trained the astronauts in one skill more than in any other: the art of *not* panicking.

When people panic, they make mistakes. They override systems. They disregard procedures, ignore rules. They deviate from the plan. They become unresponsive and stop thinking clearly. They just react—not to what they need to react to, but to the survival hormones that are coursing through their veins.

Welcome to the source of most of our problems down here on Earth. Everything is planned down to the letter, then something goes wrong and the first thing we do is trade in our plan for a good ol' emotional freak-out. Some of us almost crave sounding the alarm, because it's easier than dealing with whatever is staring us in the face.

At 150 miles above Earth in a spaceship smaller than a VW, this is death. Panic is suicide.

So panic has to be trained out. And it does not go easily.

Before the first launch, NASA re-created the fateful day for the astronauts over and over, step by step, hundreds of times—from what they'd have for breakfast to the ride to the airfield. Slowly, in a graded series of "exposures," the astronauts were introduced to every sight and sound of the experience of their firing into space. They did it so many times that it became as natural and familiar as breathing. They'd practice all the way through, holding nothing back but the liftoff itself, making sure to solve for every variable and remove all uncertainty.

Uncertainty and fear are relieved by authority. Training is authority. It's a release valve. With enough exposure, you can adapt out those perfectly ordinary, even innate, fears that are bred mostly from unfamiliarity. Fortunately, unfamiliarity is simple to fix (again, not easy), which makes it possible to increase our tolerance for stress and uncertainty.

John Glenn, the first American astronaut to orbit the earth, spent nearly a day in space still keeping his heart rate under a hundred beats per minute. That's a man not simply sitting *at* the controls but *in* control of his emotions. A man who had properly cultivated, what Tom Wolfe later called, "the Right Stuff."

But you . . . confront a client or a stranger on the street and your heart is liable to burst out of your chest; or you are called on to address a crowd and your stomach crashes through the floor.

It's time to realize that this is a luxury, an indulgence of our lesser self. In space, the difference between life and death lies in emotional regulation.

Hitting the wrong button, reading the instrument panels incorrectly, engaging a sequence too early—none of these could have been afforded on a successful Apollo mission—the consequences were too great.

Thus, the question for astronauts was not How skilled a pilot are you, but Can you keep an even strain? Can you fight the urge to panic and instead focus only on what you can change? On the task at hand?

Life is really no different. Obstacles make us emotional, but the only way we'll survive or overcome them is by keeping those emotions in check—if we can keep steady no matter what happens, no matter how much external events may fluctuate.

The Greeks had a word for this: *apatheia*.

It's the kind of calm equanimity that comes with the absence of irrational or extreme emotions. Not the loss of feeling altogether, just the loss of the harmful, unhelpful kind. Don't let the negativity in, don't let those emotions even get started. Just say: *No, thank you. I can't afford to panic.*

This is the skill that must be cultivated—freedom from disturbance and perturbation—so you can focus your energy exclusively on solving problems, rather than reacting to them.

A boss's urgent e-mail. An asshole at a bar. A call from the bank—your financing has been pulled. A knock at the door—there's been an accident.

As Gavin de Becker writes in *The Gift of Fear,* "When you worry, ask yourself, 'What am I choosing to not see right now?' What important things are you missing because you chose worry over introspection, alertness or wisdom?"

Another way of putting it: Does getting upset provide you with more options?

Sometimes it does. But in *this* instance?

No, I suppose not.

Well, then.

If an emotion can't change the condition or the situation you're dealing with, it is likely an unhelpful emotion. Or, quite possibly, a destructive one.

But it's what I feel.

Right, no one said anything about not feeling it. No one said you can't ever cry. Forget "manliness." If you need to take a moment, by all means, go ahead. Real strength lies in the *control* or, as Nassim Taleb put it, the *domestication* of one's emotions, not in pretending they don't exist.

So go ahead, feel it. Just don't lie to yourself by conflating emoting about a problem and dealing with it. Because they are as different as sleeping and waking.

You can always remind yourself: *I am in control, not my emotions. I see what's really going on here. I'm not going to get excited or upset.*

We defeat emotions with logic, or at least that's the idea. Logic is questions and statements. With enough of them, we get to root causes (which are always easier to deal with).

We lost money.

But aren't losses a pretty common part of business?

Yes.

Are these losses catastrophic?

Not necessarily.

So this is not totally unexpected, is it? How could that be so bad? Why are you all worked up over something that is at least occasionally supposed to happen?

Well . . . uhh . . . I . . .

And not only that, but you've dealt with worse situations than this. Wouldn't you be better off applying some of that resourcefulness rather than anger?

Try having that conversation with yourself and see how those extreme emotions hold up. They won't last long, trust that.

After all, you're probably not going to *die* from any of this.

It might help to say it over and over again whenever you feel the anxiety begin to come on: *I am not going to die from this. I am not going to die from this. I am not going to die from this.*

Or try Marcus's question:

> *Does what happened keep you from acting with justice, generosity, self-control, sanity, prudence, honesty, humility, straightforward-ness?*

Nope.

Then get back to work!

Subconsciously, we should be constantly asking ourselves this question: *Do I need to freak out about this?*

And the answer—like it is for astronauts, for soldiers, for doctors, and for so many other professionals—must be: *No, because I practiced for this situation and I can control myself.* Or, *No, because I caught myself and I'm able to realize that that doesn't add anything constructive.*

PRACTICE OBJECTIVITY

> Don't let the force of an impression when it first hit you
> knock you off your feet; just say to it: Hold on a moment;
> let me see who you are and what you represent. Let me
> put you to the test.
>
> —EPICTETUS

The phrase "This happened and it is bad" is actually two impressions. The first—"This happened"—is objective. The second—"it is bad"—is subjective.

The sixteenth-century Samurai swordsman Miyamoto Musashi won countless fights against feared opponents, even multiple opponents, in which he was swordless. In *The Book of Five Rings,* he notes the difference between observing and perceiving. The perceiving eye is weak, he wrote; the observing eye is strong.

Musashi understood that the observing eye sees simply what is there. The perceiving eye sees more than what is there.

The observing eye sees events, clear of distractions, exaggerations, and misperceptions. The perceiving eye sees "insurmountable obstacles" or "major setbacks" or even just "issues." It brings its own issues to the fight. The former is helpful, the latter is not.

To paraphrase Nietzsche, sometimes being superficial—taking things only at first glance—is the most profound approach.

In our own lives, how many problems seem to come from applying judgments to things we don't control, as though there were a way they were *supposed* to be? How often do we see what we think is there or should be there, instead of what actually is there?

Having steadied ourselves and held back our emotions, we can see things as they really are. We can do that using our observing eye.

Perceptions are the problem. They give us the "information" that we don't need, exactly at the moment when it would be far better to focus on what is immediately in front of us: the thrust of a sword, a crucial business negotiation, an opportunity, a flash of insight or anything else, for that matter.

Everything about our animalistic brains tries to compress the space between impression and perception. Think, perceive, act—with milliseconds between them.

A deer's brain tells it to run because things are bad. It runs. Sometimes, right into traffic.

We can question that impulse. We can disagree with it. We can override the switch, examine the threat before we act.

But this takes strength. It's a muscle that must be developed. And muscles are developed by tension, by lifting and holding.

This is why Musashi and most martial arts practitioners focus on mental training as much as on physical training. Both are equally important—and require equally vigorous exercise and practice.

In the writings of the Stoics we see an exercise that might well be described as Contemptuous Expressions. The Stoics use contempt as an agent to lay things bare and *"to strip away the legend that encrusts them."*

Epictetus told his students, when they'd quote some great thinker, to picture themselves observing the person having sex. It's funny, you should try it the next time someone intimidates you or makes you feel insecure. See them in your mind, grunting, groaning, and awkward in their private life—just like the rest of us.

Marcus Aurelius had a version of this exercise where he'd describe glamorous or expensive things without their euphemisms—roasted meat is a dead animal and vintage wine is old, fermented grapes. The aim was to see these things as they really are, without any of the ornamentation.

We can do this for anyone or to anything that stands in our way. That promotion that means so much, what is it really? Our critics and naysayers who make us feel small, let's put them in their proper place. It's so much better to see things as they truly, actually are, not as we've made them in our minds.

Objectivity means removing "you"—the subjective part—from the equation. Just think, what happens when we give others advice? Their problems are crystal clear to us, the solutions obvious. Something that's present when we deal with our own obstacles is always missing when we hear other people's problems: the baggage. With other people we can be objective.

We take the situation at face value and immediately set about helping our friend to solve it. Selfishly—and stupidly—we save the pity and the sense of persecution and the complaints for our own lives.

Take your situation and pretend it is not happening to you. Pretend it is not important, that it doesn't matter. How much easier would it be for you to know what to do? How much more quickly and dispassionately could you size up the scenario and its options? You could write it off, greet it calmly.

Think of all the ways that someone could solve a specific problem. No, *really* think. Give yourself clarity, not sympathy—there'll be plenty of time for that later. It's an exercise, which means it takes repetition. The more you try it, the better you get at it. The more skilled you become seeing things for what they are, the more perception will work for you rather than against you.

ALTER YOUR PERSPECTIVE

Man does not simply exist but always decides what his
existence will be, what he will become the next moment.
By the same token, every human being has the freedom
to change at any instant.

—VIKTOR FRANKL

Once as the Athenian general Pericles cast off on a naval
mission in the Peloponnesian War, the sun was eclipsed
and his fleet of 150 ships was cast into darkness.

Surprised by this unexpected and confusing event, his
men were thrown into a state of panic. Unlike the crew, Pericles was undaunted. He walked up to a lead steersman, re-
moved the cloak he was wearing, and held it up around the
man's face. He asked the man if he was scared of what he saw.

No, of course not.

So what does it matter, Pericles replied, when the cause of
the darkness differs?

The Greeks were clever. But beneath this particular quip
is the fundamental notion that girds not just Stoic philosophy but cognitive psychology: *Perspective is everything.*

That is, when you can break apart something, or look at it
from some new angle, it loses its power over you.

Fear is debilitating, distracting, tiring, and often irrational. Pericles understood this completely, and he was able to use the power of perspective to defeat it.

The Greeks understood that we often choose the ominous explanation over the simple one, to our detriment. That we are scared of obstacles because our perspective is wrong—that a simple shift in perspective can change our reaction entirely. The task, as Pericles showed, is not to ignore fear but to explain it away. Take what you're afraid of—when fear strikes you—and break it apart.

Remember: We choose how we'll look at things. We retain the ability to inject perspective into a situation. We can't change the obstacles themselves—that part of the equation is set—but the power of perspective can change how the obstacles appear. How we approach, view, and contextualize an obstacle, and what we tell ourselves it means, determines how daunting and trying it will be to overcome.

It's your choice whether you want to put *I* in front of something (I *hate public speaking.* I *screwed up.* I *am harmed by this*). These add an extra element: *you* in relation to that obstacle, rather than just the obstacle itself. And with the wrong perspective, we become consumed and overwhelmed with something actually quite small. So why subject ourselves to that?

The right perspective has a strange way of cutting obstacles—and adversity—down to size.

But for whatever reason, we tend to look at things in isolation. We kick ourselves for blowing a deal or having to miss a meeting. Individually, that does suck—we just missed 100 percent of that opportunity.

What we're forgetting in that instance, as billionaire serial entrepreneur Richard Branson likes to say, is that "business opportunities are like buses; there's always another coming around." One meeting is nothing in a lifetime of meetings, one deal is just one deal. In fact, we may have actually dodged a bullet. The next opportunity might be better.

The way we look out at the world changes how we see these things. Is our perspective truly giving us *perspective* or is it what's actually causing the problem? That's the question.

What we can do is limit and expand our perspective to whatever will keep us calmest and most ready for the task at hand. Think of it as selective editing—not to deceive others, but to properly orient ourselves.

And it *works*. Small tweaks can change what once felt like impossible tasks. Suddenly, where we felt weak, we realize we are strong. With perspective, we discover leverage we didn't know we had.

Perspective has two definitions.

1. Context: a sense of the larger picture of the world, not just what is immediately in front of us
2. Framing: an individual's unique way of looking at the world, a way that interprets its events

Both matter, both can be effectively injected to change a situation that previously seemed intimidating or impossible.

George Clooney spent his first years in Hollywood getting rejected at auditions. He wanted the producers and directors to like him, but they didn't and it hurt and he blamed the system for not seeing how good he was.

This perspective should sound familiar. It's the dominant

viewpoint for the rest of us on job interviews, when we pitch clients, or try to connect with an attractive stranger in a coffee shop. We subconsciously submit to what Seth Godin, author and entrepreneur, refers to as the "tyranny of being picked."

Everything changed for Clooney when he tried a new perspective. He realized that casting is an obstacle for producers, too—they *need* to find somebody, and they're all hoping that the next person to walk in the room is the *right* somebody. Auditions were a chance to solve their problem, not his.

From Clooney's new perspective, he was that solution. He wasn't going to be someone groveling for a shot. He was someone with something special to offer. He was the answer to their prayers, not the other way around. That was what he began projecting in his auditions—not exclusively his acting skills but that he was the man for the job. That he understood what the casting director and producers were looking for in a specific role and that he would deliver it in each and every situation, in preproduction, on camera, and during promotion.

The difference between the right and the wrong perspective is everything.

How we interpret the events in our lives, our perspective, is the framework for our forthcoming response—whether there will even be one or whether we'll just lie there and take it.

Where the head goes, the body follows. Perception precedes action. Right action follows the right perspective.

IS IT UP TO YOU?

In life our first job is this, to divide and distinguish things
into two categories: externals I cannot control, but the choices
I make with regard to them I do control. Where will I find good
and bad? In me, in my choices.

—EPICTETUS

Tommy John, one of baseball's most savvy and durable
pitchers, played twenty-six seasons in the majors.
Twenty-six seasons! His rookie year, Kennedy was president.
His final year, it was George H. W. Bush. He pitched to
Mickey Mantle *and* Mark McGwire.

It's an almost superhuman accomplishment. But he was
able to do it because he got really good at asking himself
and others, in various forms, one question over and over
again: *Is there a chance? Do I have a shot? Is there something I can
do?*

All he ever looked for was a yes, no matter how slight or
tentative or provisional the chance. If there was a chance, he
was ready to take it and make good use of it—ready to give
every ounce of effort and energy he had to make it happen.
If effort would affect the outcome, he would die on the field
before he let that chance go to waste.

The first time came during the middle of the 1974 season when Tommy John blew out his arm, permanently damaging the ulnar collateral ligament in his pitching elbow. Up until this point in baseball and sports medicine, when a pitcher blew out his arm that was it. They called it a "dead arm" injury. Game over.

John wouldn't accept that. Was there *anything* that could give him a shot to get back on the mound? It turns out there was. The doctors suggested an experimental surgery in which they would try to replace the ligament in his pitching elbow with a tendon from his other arm. *What are the chances of me coming back after this surgery?* One in one hundred. And without it? *No chance,* they said.

He could have retired. But there was a one in one hundred chance. With rehab and training, the opportunity was *partially* in his control. He took it. And won 164 more games over the next thirteen seasons. That procedure is now famously known as Tommy John surgery.

Less than ten years later, John mustered the same spirit and effort he marshaled for his elbow surgery when his young son fell horrifyingly from a third-story window, swallowed his tongue, and nearly died. Even in the chaos of the emergency room, with doctors convinced that the boy probably wouldn't survive, John reminded his family that whether it took one year or ten years, they wouldn't give up until there was absolutely nothing left that they could do.

His son made a full recovery.

For John, his baseball career seemed to finally come to an end in 1988, when, at the age of forty-five, he was cut by the Yankees at the end of the season. Still, he would not accept it. He called the coach and demanded: If he showed up at spring training as a walk-on the next spring, would he get a fair look? They replied that he shouldn't be playing baseball at his age. He repeated the question: *Be straight with me, if I come down there, would I have a chance?* The baseball officials answered, *Fine, yes, you'll get one look.*

So Tommy John was the first to report to camp. He trained many hours a day, brought every lesson he'd learned playing the sport for a quarter century, and made the team—as the oldest player in the game. He started the season opener—and won, giving up a scant two runs over seven innings on the road at Minnesota.

The things that Tommy John could change—when he had a chance—got a full 100 percent of the effort he could muster. He used to tell coaches that he would die on the field before he quit. He understood that as a professional athlete his job was to parse the difference between the unlikely and the impossible. Seeing that minuscule distinction was what made him who he was.

To harness the same power, recovering addicts learn the Serenity Prayer.

> *God, grant me the serenity to accept the things I cannot change*
> *The courage to change the things I can,*
> *And the wisdom to know the difference.*

This is how they focus their efforts. It's a lot easier to fight addiction when you aren't also fighting the fact that you were born, that your parents were monsters, or that you lost everything. That stuff is done. Delivered. Zero in one hundred chances that you can change it.

So what if you focused on what you *can* change? That's where you can make a difference.

Behind the Serenity Prayer is a two-thousand-year-old Stoic phrase: *"ta eph'hemin, ta ouk eph'hemin."* What is up to us, what is not up to us.

And what is up to us?

Our emotions
Our judgments
Our creativity
Our attitude
Our perspective
Our desires
Our decisions
Our determination

This is our playing field, so to speak. Everything there is fair game.

What is not up to us?

Well, you know, everything else. The weather, the economy, circumstances, other people's emotions or judgments, trends, disasters, et cetera.

If what's up to us is the playing field, then what is not up to us are the rules and conditions of the game. Factors that winning athletes make the best of and don't spend time arguing against (because there is no point).

To argue, to complain, or worse, to just give up, these are choices. Choices that more often than not, do *nothing* to get us across the finish line.

When it comes to perception, this is the crucial distinction to make: the difference between the things that are in our power and the things that aren't. That's the difference between the people who can accomplish great things, and the people who find it impossible to stay sober—to avoid not just drugs or alcohol but *all* addictions.

In its own way, the most harmful dragon we chase is the one that makes us think we can change things that are simply not ours to change. That someone decided not to fund your company, this isn't up to you. But the decision to refine and improve your pitch? That is. That someone stole your idea or got to it first? No. To pivot, improve it, or fight for what's yours? Yes.

Focusing exclusively on what is in our power magnifies and enhances our power. But every ounce of energy directed at things we can't actually influence is wasted—self-indulgent and self-destructive. So much power—ours, and other people's—is frittered away in this manner.

To see an obstacle as a challenge, to make the best of it anyway, that is also a choice—a choice that is *up to us*.

Will I have a chance, Coach?

Ta eph'hemin?

Is this up to me?

LIVE IN THE PRESENT MOMENT

The trick to forgetting the big picture is to look
at everything close up.

—CHUCK PALAHNIUK

D o yourself a favor and run down the list of businesses
started during depressions or economic crises.

Fortune magazine (ninety days after the market crash
of 1929)
FedEx (oil crisis of 1973)
UPS (Panic of 1907)
Walt Disney Company (After eleven months of
smooth operation, the twelfth was the market
crash of 1929.)
Hewlett-Packard (Great Depression, 1935)
Charles Schwab (market crash of 1974–75)
Standard Oil (Rockefeller bought out his partners in
what became Standard Oil and took over in
February 1865, the final year of the Civil War.)
Coors (Depression of 1873)
Costco (recession in the late 1970s)
Revlon (Great Depression, 1932)

General Motors (Panic of 1907)
Proctor & Gamble (Panic of 1837)
United Airlines (1929)
Microsoft (recession in 1973–75)
LinkedIn (2002, post–dot-com bubble)

For the most part, these businesses had little awareness they were in some historically significant depression. Why? Because the founders were too busy existing in the present—actually dealing with the situation at hand. They didn't know whether it would get better or worse, they just knew what *was*. They had a job they wanted to do, a great idea they believed in or a product they thought they could sell. They knew they had payroll to meet.

Yet in our own lives, we aren't content to deal with things as they happen. We have to dive endlessly into what everything "means," whether something is "fair" or not, what's "behind" this or that, and what everyone else is doing. Then we wonder why we don't have the energy to actually deal with our problems. Or we get ourselves so worked up and intimidated because of the overthinking, that if we'd just gotten to work we'd probably be done already.

Our understanding of the world of business is all mixed up with storytelling and mythology. Which is funny because we're missing the real story by focusing on individuals. In fact, half the companies in the Fortune 500 were started during a bear market or recession. *Half.*

The point is that *most people* start from disadvantage (often with no idea they are doing so) and do just fine. It's not unfair, it's universal. Those who survive it, survive because they took things day by day—that's the real secret.

Focus on the moment, not the monsters that may or may not be up ahead.

A business must take the operating constraints of the world around it as a given and work for whatever gains are possible. Those people with an entrepreneurial spirit are like animals, blessed to have no time and no ability to think about the ways things should be, or how they'd prefer them to be.

For all species other than us humans, things just are what they are. Our problem is that we're always trying to figure out what things *mean*—why things are the way they are. As though the *why* matters. Emerson put it best: "We cannot spend the day in explanation." Don't waste time on false constructs.

It doesn't matter whether this is the worst time to be alive or the best, whether you're in a good job market or a bad one, or that the obstacle you face is intimidating or burdensome. What matters is that right now is right now.

The implications of our obstacle are theoretical—they exist in the past and the future. We live *in the moment*. And the more we embrace that, the easier the obstacle will be to face and move.

You can take the trouble you're dealing with and use it as an opportunity to focus on the present moment. To ignore the totality of your situation and learn to be content with what happens, as it happens. To have no "way" that the future needs to be to confirm your predictions, because you didn't make any. To let each new moment be a refresh wiping clear what came before and what others were hoping would come next.

You'll find the method that works best for you, but there are many things that can pull you into the present moment:

Strenuous exercise. Unplugging. A walk in the park. Meditation. Getting a dog—they're a constant reminder of how pleasant the present is.

One thing is certain. It's not simply a matter of saying: *Oh, I'll live in the present.* You have to *work* at it. Catch your mind when it wanders—don't let it get away from you. Discard distracting thoughts. Leave things well enough alone—no matter how much you feel like doing otherwise.

But it's easier when the choice to limit your scope feels like editing rather than acting. Remember that this moment is not your life, it's just a moment *in* your life. Focus on what is in front of you, right now. Ignore what it "represents" or it "means" or "why it happened to you."

There is plenty else going on right here to care about any of that.

THINK DIFFERENTLY

Genius is the ability to put into effect what is in your mind.
There's no other definition of it.

—F. SCOTT FITZGERALD

Steve Jobs was famous for what observers called his "reality distortion field." Part motivational tactic, part sheer drive and ambition, this field made him notoriously dismissive of phrases such as "It can't be done" or "We need more time."

Having learned early in life that reality was falsely hemmed in by rules and compromises that people had been taught as children, Jobs had a much more aggressive idea of what was or wasn't possible. To him, when you factored in vision and work ethic, much of life was malleable.

For instance, in the design stages for a new mouse for an early Apple product, Jobs had high expectations. He wanted it to move fluidly in any direction—a new development for any mouse at that time—but a lead engineer was told by one of his designers that this would be commercially impossible. What Jobs wanted wasn't realistic and wouldn't work. The next day, the lead engineer arrived at work to find that Steve Jobs had fired the employee who'd said that. When the replacement came in, his first words were: "I can build the mouse."

This was Jobs's view of reality at work. Malleable, adamant, self-confident. Not in the delusional sense, but for the purposes of accomplishing something. He knew that to aim low meant to accept mediocre accomplishment. But a high aim could, if things went right, create something extraordinary. He was Napoleon shouting to his soldiers: "There shall be no Alps!"

For most of us, such confidence does not come easy. It's understandable. So many people in our lives have preached the need to be realistic or conservative or worse—to not rock the boat. This is an enormous disadvantage when it comes to trying big things. Because though our doubts (and self-doubts) feel real, they have very little bearing on what is and isn't possible.

Our perceptions determine, to an incredibly large degree, what we are and are not capable of. In many ways, they determine reality itself. When we believe in the obstacle more than in the goal, which will inevitably triumph?

For instance, think of artists. It's their unique vision and voice that push the definition of "art" forward. What was possible for an artist before Caravaggio and after he stunned us with his dark masterpieces were two very different things. Plug in any other thinker or writer or painter in their own time, and the same applies.

This is why we shouldn't listen too closely to what other people say (or to what the voice in our head says, either). We'll find ourselves erring on the side of accomplishing nothing.

Be open. Question.

Though of course we don't *control* reality, our perceptions do influence it.

One week before the first Macintosh computer was supposed to ship, the engineers told Jobs they couldn't make the deadline. On a hastily assembled conference call, the engineers explained that they needed just two additional weeks' work before it was ready. Jobs responded calmly, explaining to the engineers that if they could make it in two weeks, they could surely make it one—there was no real difference in such a short period of time. And, more important, since they'd come this far and done so much good work, there was no way they would *not* ship on January 16, the original ship date. The engineers rallied and made their deadline. His insistence pushed them, once again, past what they ever thought possible.

Now, how do you and I usually deal with an impossible deadline handed down from someone above us? We complain. We get angry. We question. *How could they? What's the point? Who do they think I am?* We look for a way out and feel sorry for ourselves.

Of course, none of these things affect the objective reality of that deadline. Not in the way that pushing forward can. Jobs refused to tolerate people who didn't believe in their own abilities to succeed. Even if his demands were unfair, uncomfortable, or ambitious.

The genius and wonder of his products—which often felt impossibly intuitive and futuristic—embody that trait. He had pushed through what others thought were hard limitations and, as a result, he created something totally new. No one believed Apple could make the products it made. In fact, Jobs was pushed out in 1985 because the board members at that time felt that Apple's foray into consumer products was a "lunatic plan." Of course, they were wrong.

Jobs learned to reject the first judgments and the objections that spring out of them because those objections are almost always rooted in fear. When he ordered a special kind of glass for the first iPhone, the manufacturer was aghast at the aggressive deadline. "We don't have capacity," they said. "Don't be afraid," Jobs replied. "You can do it. Get your mind around it. You can do it." Nearly overnight, manufacturers transformed their facilities into glass-making behemoths, and within six months they'd made enough for the whole first run of the phone.

This is radically different from how we've been taught to act. *Be realistic,* we're told. *Listen to feedback. Play well with others. Compromise.* Well, what if the "other" party is wrong? What if conventional wisdom is too conservative? It's this all-too-common impulse to *complain, defer, and then give up* that holds us back.

An entrepreneur is someone with faith in their ability to make something where there was nothing before. To them, the idea that no one has *ever* done this or that is a good thing. When given an unfair task, some rightly see it as a chance to test what they're made of—to give it all they've got, knowing full well how difficult it will be to win. They see it as an opportunity because it is often in that desperate nothing-to-lose state that we are our most creative.

Our best ideas come from there, where obstacles illuminate new options.

FINDING THE OPPORTUNITY

*A good person dyes events with his own color . . . and turns
whatever happens to his own benefit.*

—SENECA

One of the most intimidating and shocking develop-
ments in modern warfare was the German Blitzkrieg
(lightning war). In World War II the Germans wanted to
avoid the drawn-out trench fighting of previous wars. So
they concentrated mobile divisions into rapid, narrow offensive forces that caught their enemies completely unprepared.

Like the tip of a spear, columns of panzer tanks rushed
into Poland, the Netherlands, Belgium, and France with
devastating results and little opposition. In most cases, the
opposing commanders simply surrendered rather than face
what felt like an invincible, indefatigable monster bearing
down on them. The Blitzkrieg strategy was designed to ex-
ploit the flinch of the enemy—he must collapse at the sight
of what appears to be overwhelming force. Its success de-
pends completely on this response. This military strategy
works because the set-upon troops see the offensive force as
an enormous obstacle bearing down on them.

This is how the Allied opposition regarded the Blitzkrieg

for most of the war. They could see only its power, and their own vulnerability to it. In the weeks and months after the successful invasion of Normandy by Allied forces, they faced it again: a set of massive German counteroffensives. How could they stop it? Would it throw them back to the very beaches they just purchased at such high cost?

A great leader answered that question. Striding into the conference room at headquarters in Malta, General Dwight D. Eisenhower made an announcement: He'd have no more of this quivering timidity from his deflated generals. "The present situation is to be regarded as opportunity for us and not disaster," he commanded. "There will be only cheerful faces at this conference table."

In the surging counteroffensive, Eisenhower was able to see the tactical solution that had been in front of them the entire time: the Nazi strategy carried its own destruction within itself.

Only then were the Allies able to see the opportunity *inside* the obstacle rather than simply the obstacle that threatened them. Properly seen, as long as the Allies could bend and not break, this attack would send more than fifty thousand Germans rushing headfirst into a net—or a "meat grinder," as Patton eloquently put it.

The Battle of the Bulge and before that the Battle of the Falaise Pocket, both of which were feared to be major reversals and the end of the Allies' momentum, in fact were their greatest triumphs. By allowing a forward wedge of the German army through and then attacking from the sides, the Allies encircled the enemy completely from the rear. The invincible, penetrating thrust of the German Panzers wasn't just impotent but suicidal—a textbook example of why you never leave your flanks exposed.

More important, it's a textbook example of the role our own perceptions play in the success or failures of those who oppose us.

It's one thing to not be overwhelmed by obstacles, or discouraged or upset by them. This is something that few are able to do. But after you have controlled your emotions, and you can see objectively and stand steadily, the next step becomes possible: a mental flip, so you're looking not at the obstacle but at the opportunity within it.

As Laura Ingalls Wilder put it: "There is good in everything, if only we look for it."

Yet we are so bad at looking. We close our eyes to the gift. Imagine if you'd been in Eisenhower's shoes, with an army racing toward you, and you could see only impending defeat. How much longer would the war have gone on? How many more lives lost?

It's our preconceptions that are the problem. They tell us that things should or need to be a certain way, so when they're not, we naturally assume that we are at a disadvantage or that we'd be wasting our time to pursue an alternate course. When really, it's all fair game, and every situation is an opportunity for us to act.

Let's take a circumstance we've all been in: having a bad boss. All we see is the hell. All we see is that thing bearing down on us. We flinch.

But what if you regarded it as an opportunity instead of a disaster?

If you mean it when you say you're at the end of your rope

and would rather quit, you actually have a unique chance to grow and improve yourself. A unique opportunity to experiment with different solutions, to try different tactics, or to take on new projects to add to your skill set. You can study this bad boss and learn from him—while you fill out your résumé and hit up contacts for a better job elsewhere. You can prepare yourself for that job by trying new styles of communication or standing up for yourself, all with a perfect safety net for yourself: quitting and getting out of there.

With this new attitude and fearlessness, who knows, you might be able to extract concessions and find that you like the job again. One day, the boss will make a mistake, and then you'll make your move and outmaneuver them. It will feel so much better than the alternative—whining, badmouthing, duplicity, spinelessness.

Or take that longtime rival at work (or that rival company), the one who causes endless headaches? Note the fact that they also:

- keep you alert
- raise the stakes
- motivate you to prove them wrong
- harden you
- help you to appreciate true friends
- provide an instructive antilog—an example of whom you don't want to become

Or that computer glitch that erased all your work? You will now be twice as good at it since you will do it again.

How about that business decision that turned out to be a mistake? Well, you had a hypothesis and it turned out to be wrong. Why should that upset you? It wouldn't piss off a scientist, it would *help* him. Maybe don't bet so much on it next time. And now you've learned two things: that your instinct was wrong, and the kind of appetite for risk you really have.

Blessings and burdens are not mutually exclusive. It's a lot more complicated. Socrates had a mean, nagging wife; he always said that being married to her was good practice for philosophy.

Of course you'd want to avoid something negative if you could. But what if you were able to remember, in the moment, the second act that seems to come with the unfortunate situations we try so hard to avoid?

Sports psychologists recently did a study of elite athletes who were struck with some adversity or serious injury. Initially, each reported feeling isolation, emotional disruption, and doubts about their athletic ability. Yet afterward, each reported gaining a desire to help others, additional perspective, and realization of their own strengths. In other words, every fear and doubt they felt during the injury turned into greater abilities in those exact areas.

It's a beautiful idea. Psychologists call it adversarial growth and post-traumatic growth. "That which doesn't kill me makes me stronger" is not a cliché but fact.

The struggle against an obstacle inevitably propels the fighter to a new level of functioning. The extent of the struggle determines the extent of the growth. The obstacle is an advantage, not adversity. The enemy is any perception that prevents us from seeing this.

Of all the strategies we've talked about, this is the one you can always use. Everything can be flipped, seen with this kind of gaze: a piercing look that ignores the package and sees only the gift.

Or we can fight it the entire way. The result is the same. The obstacle still exists. One just hurts less. The benefit is still there below the surface. What kind of idiot decides not to take it?

Now the things that other people avoid, or flinch away from, we're thankful for.

When people are:

—rude or disrespectful:

They underestimate us. A huge advantage.

—conniving:

We won't have to apologize when we make an example out of them.

—critical or question our abilities:

Lower expectations are easier to exceed.

—lazy:

Makes whatever we accomplish seem all the more admirable.

It's striking: These are perfectly fine starting points, better, in some cases, than whatever you'd have hoped for in the best scenario. What advantage do you derive from someone being polite? Or pulling their punches? Behind the behaviors that provoke an immediate negative reaction is opportunity—some exposed benefit that we can seize mentally and then act upon.

So focus on that—on the poorly wrapped and initially repulsive present you've been handed in every seemingly disadvantageous situation. Because beneath the packaging is what we need—often something of real value. A gift of great benefit.

No one is talking glass-half-full-style platitudes here. This must be a complete flip. Seeing through the negative, past its underside, and into its corollary: the positive.

PREPARE TO ACT

> Then imitate the action of the tiger;
> stiffen the sinews, summon up the blood.
>
> —SHAKESPEARE

Problems are rarely as bad as we think—or rather, they are *precisely* as bad as we *think*.

It's a huge step forward to realize that the worst thing to happen is never the event, but the event *and* losing your head. Because then you'll have two problems (one of them unnecessary and post hoc).

The demand on you is this: Once you see the world as it is, for what it is, you must act. The proper perception—objective, rational, ambitious, clean—isolates the obstacle and exposes it for what it is.

A clearer head makes for steadier hands.

And then those hands must be put to work. *Good* use.

We all have to make assumptions in life, we have to weigh the costs and benefits. No one is asking you to look at the world through rose-colored glasses. No one is asking for noble failure or martyrdom.

But *boldness* is acting anyway, even though you understand the negative and the reality of your obstacle. Decide to

tackle what stands in your way—not because you're a gam-
bler defying the odds but because you've calculated them
and boldly embraced the risk.

After all, now that you've managed perceptions properly,
what's next is to act.

Are you ready?

PART II

Action

WHAT IS ACTION? Action is commonplace, right action is not. As a discipline, it's not any kind of action that will do, but *directed* action. Everything must be done in the service of the whole. Step by step, action by action, we'll dismantle the obstacles in front of us. With persistence and flexibility, we'll act in the best interest of our goals. Action requires courage, not brashness—creative application and not brute force. Our movements and decisions define us: We must be sure to act with deliberation, boldness, and persistence. Those are the attributes of right and effective action. Nothing else— not thinking or evasion or aid from others. Action is the solution and the cure to our predicaments.

THE DISCIPLINE OF ACTION

There was little evidence that Demosthenes was destined to become the greatest orator of Athens, let alone all of history. He was born sickly and frail with a nearly debilitating speech impediment. At seven years old, he lost his father. And then things got worse.

The large inheritance left to him—intended to pay for tutors and the best schools—was stolen by the guardians entrusted to protect him. They refused to pay his tutors, depriving him of the education he was entitled to. Still weak and sick, Demosthenes was also unable to distinguish himself in the other critical sphere of Greek life: the floor of the gymnasia.

Here was this fatherless, effeminate, awkward child who no one understood, who everyone laughed at. Not exactly the boy you'd expect would soon hold the power to mobilize a nation to war by his voice alone.

Disadvantaged by nature, abandoned by the people he depended on, nearly every wrong that can be inflicted on a child befell Demosthenes. None of it was fair, none of it was right. Most of us, were we in his position, would have given up right then and there. But Demosthenes did not.

Stuck in his young mind was the image of a great orator, a man he'd once witnessed speaking at the court at Athens. This lone individual, so skilled and powerful, had held the admiration of the crowd, who hung on his every word for hours—subduing all opposition with no more than the sound of his voice and the strength of his ideas. It inspired and challenged Demosthenes, weak, beaten on, powerless, and ignored; for in many ways, this strong, confident speaker was the opposite of him.

So he did something about it.

To conquer his speech impediment, he devised his own strange exercises. He would fill his mouth with pebbles and practice speaking. He rehearsed full speeches into the wind or while running up steep inclines. He learned to give entire speeches with a single breath. And soon, his quiet, weak voice erupted with booming, powerful clarity.

Demosthenes locked himself away underground—literally—in a dugout he'd had built in which to study and educate himself. To ensure he wouldn't indulge in outside distractions, he shaved half his head so he'd be too embarrassed to go outside. And from that point forward, he dutifully descended each day into his study to work with his voice, his facial expressions, and his arguments.

When he did venture out, it was to learn even more. Every moment, every conversation, every transaction, was an opportunity for him to improve his art. All of it aimed at one goal: to face his enemies in court and win back what had been taken from him. Which he did.

When he came of age, he finally filed suits against the negligent guardians who had wronged him. They evaded his efforts and hired their own lawyers, but he refused to be stopped. Flexible and creative, he matched them suit for suit and delivered countless speeches. Confident in his new strengths, driven on by his own toil, they were no match. Demosthenes eventually won.

Only a fraction of the original inheritance remained, but the money had become secondary. Demosthenes's reputation as an orator, ability to command a crowd and his peerless knowledge of the intricacies of the law, was worth more than whatever remained of a once-great fortune.

Every speech he delivered made him stronger, every day that he stuck with it made him more determined. He could see through bullies and stare down fear. In struggling with his unfortunate fate, Demosthenes found his true calling: He would be the voice of Athens, its great speaker and conscience. He would be successful precisely because of what he'd been through and how he'd reacted to it. He had channeled his rage and pain into his training, and then later into his speeches, fueling it all with a kind of fierceness and power that could be neither matched nor resisted.

Some academic once asked Demosthenes what the three most important traits of speechmaking were. His reply says it all: "Action, Action, Action!"

Sure, Demosthenes lost the inheritance he'd been born with, and that was unfortunate. But in the process of dealing with this reality, he created a far better one—one that could never be taken from him.

But you, when you're dealt a bad hand. What's your response? Do you fold? Or do you play it for all you've got?

There's an explosion, metaphoric or otherwise. Are you the guy running toward it? Or running away from it? Or worse, are you paralyzed and do nothing?

This little test of character says everything about us.

And it's sad that so many of us fail—opting away from action. Because action is natural, innate. You trip and fall right now, your body's instincts protect you. You extend your hands to break your fall, so you don't break your face. In a vicious accident, you go into shock but still manage to get your arms up around your face. That's where the term *defensive wounds* comes from. We don't think, we don't complain, we don't argue. We act. We have real strength—more strength than we know.

But in our lives, when our worst instincts are in control, we dally. We don't act like Demosthenes, we act frail and are powerless to make ourselves better. We may be able to articulate a problem, even potential solutions, but then weeks, months, or sometimes years later, the problem is still there. Or it's gotten worse. As though we expect someone else to handle it, as though we honestly believe that there is a chance of obstacles *unobstacle-ing* themselves.

We've all done it. Said: "I am so [overwhelmed, tired, stressed, busy, blocked, outmatched]."

And then what do we do about it? Go out and party. Or treat ourselves. Or sleep in. Or wait.

It feels better to ignore or pretend. But you know deep down that that isn't going to truly make it any better. You've got to act. And you've got to start now.

We forget: In life, it doesn't matter what happens to you or where you came from. It matters what you do with what happens and what you've been given. And the only way you'll do something spectacular is by using it all to your advantage.

People turn shit into sugar all the time—shit that's a lot worse than whatever we're dealing with. I'm talking physical disabilities, racial discrimination, battles against overwhelmingly superior armies. But those people didn't quit. They didn't feel sorry for themselves. They didn't delude themselves with fantasies about easy solutions. They focused on the one thing that mattered: applying themselves with gusto and creativity.

Born with nothing, into poverty, strife, or the chaos of decades past, certain types of people were freed from modern notions of fairness or good or bad. Because none of it applied to them. What was in front of them was all they knew—all they had. And instead of complaining, they worked with it. They made the best of it. Because they had to, because they didn't have a choice.

No one wants to be born weak or to be victimized. No one wants to be down to their last dollar. No one wants to be stuck behind an obstacle, blocked from where they need to go. Such circumstances are not impressed by perception, but they are not indifferent—or rather immune—from action. In fact, that's the only thing these situations will respond to.

No one is saying you can't take a minute to think, *Dammit, this sucks.* By all means, vent. Exhale. Take stock. Just don't take too long. Because you have to get back to work. Because each obstacle we overcome makes us stronger for the next one.

But . . .

No. No excuses. No exceptions. No way around it: It's on you.

We don't have the luxury of running away. Of hiding. Because we have something very specific we're trying to do. We have an obstacle we have to lean into and transform.

No one is coming to save you. And if we'd like to go where we claim we want to go—to accomplish what we claim are our goals—there is only one way. And that's to meet our problems with the right action.

Therefore, we can always (and only) greet our obstacles

- with energy
- with persistence
- with a coherent and deliberate process
- with iteration and resilience
- with pragmatism
- with strategic vision
- with craftiness and savvy
- and an eye for opportunity and pivotal moments

Are you ready to get to work?

GET MOVING

We must all either wear out or rust out, every one of us.
My choice is to wear out.

—THEODORE ROOSEVELT

Amelia Earhart wanted to be a great aviator. But it was the 1920s, and people still thought that women were frail and weak and didn't have the stuff. Woman suffrage was not even a decade old.

She couldn't make her living as a pilot, so she took a job as a social worker. Then one day the phone rang. The man on the line had a pretty offensive proposition, along the lines of: *We have someone willing to fund the first female transatlantic flight. Our first choice has already backed out. You won't get to actually fly the plane, and we're going to send two men along as chaperones and guess what, we'll pay them a lot of money and you won't get anything. Oh, and you very well might die while doing it.*

You know what she said to that offer? She said *yes*.

Because that's what people who defy the odds do. That's how people who become great at things—whether it's flying or blowing through gender stereotypes—do. They start. Anywhere. Anyhow. They don't care if the conditions are perfect or if they're being slighted. Because they know that once they get started, if they can just get some momentum, they can make it work.

As it went for Amelia Earhart. Less than five years later she was the first woman to fly solo nonstop across the Atlantic and became, rightly, one of the most famous and respected people in the world.

But none of that would have happened had she turned up her nose at that offensive offer or sat around feeling sorry for herself. None of it could have happened if she'd stopped after that first accomplishment either. What mattered was that she took the opening and then pressed ahead. That was the reason for her success.

Life can be frustrating. Oftentimes we know what our problems are. We may even know what to do about them. But we fear that taking action is too risky, that we don't have the experience or that it's not how we pictured it or because it's too expensive, because it's too soon, because we think something better might come along, because it might not work.

And you know what happens as a result? Nothing. We do nothing.

Tell yourself: The time for that has passed. The wind is rising. The bell's been rung. Get started, get moving.

We often assume that the world moves at our leisure. We delay when we should initiate. We jog when we should be running or, better yet, sprinting. And then we're shocked—*shocked!*—when nothing big ever happens, when opportunities never show up, when new obstacles begin to pile up, or the enemies finally get their act together.

Of course they did, we gave them room to breathe. We gave them the chance.

So the first step is: Take the bat off your shoulder and give it a swing. You've got to start, to go anywhere.

Now let's say you've already done that. Fantastic. You're already ahead of most people. But let's ask an honest question: Could you be doing more? You probably could—there's always more. At minimum, you could be trying harder. You might have gotten started, but your full effort isn't in it—and that shows.

Is that going to affect your results? No question.

In the first years of World War II, there was no worse assignment for British troops than being sent to the North African front. Methodical and orderly, the British hated the grueling weather and terrain that wreaked havoc on their machines and their plans. They acted how they felt: slow, timid, cautious.

German Field Marshal General Erwin Rommel, on the other hand, loved it. He saw war as a game. A dangerous, reckless, untidy, fast-paced game. And, most important, he took to this game with incredible energy and was perennially pushing his troops forward.

The German troops had a saying about him: Where Rommel is, there is the front.

That's the next step: ramming your feet into the stirrups and really *going* for it.

That's definitely not what they say about most leaders today. While overpaid CEOs take long vacations and hide behind e-mail autoresponders, some programmer is working eighteen-hour days coding the start-up that will destroy that CEO's business. And if we were honest, we're probably closer to the former than the latter when it comes to the problems we face (or don't face).

While you're sleeping, traveling, attending meetings, or messing around online, the same thing is happening to you. You're going soft. You're not aggressive enough. You're not pressing ahead. You've got a million reasons why you can't move at a faster pace. This all makes the obstacles in your life loom very large.

For some reason, these days we tend to downplay the importance of aggression, of taking risks, of barreling forward. It's probably because it's been negatively associated with certain notions of violence or masculinity.

But of course Earhart shows that that isn't true. In fact, on the side of her plane she painted the words, "Always think with your stick forward." That is: You can't ever let up your flying speed—if you do, you crash. Be deliberate, of course, but you always need to be moving forward.

And that's the final part: Stay moving, *always*.

Like Earhart, Rommel knew from history that those who attack problems and life with the most initiative and energy usually win. He was always pushing ahead, keeping the stampede on the more cautious British forces to devastating effect.

His string of offensives at Cyrenaica, Tobruk, and Tunisia led to some of the most astonishing victories in the history of warfare. He got started early, while the British were still trying to get comfortable, and as a result, Rommel was able to seize what appeared to be an unstoppable advantage in some of the most uninhabitable terrain on the planet. He blew right through the bleak battlefields of North Africa, with its enormous distances, blinding sandstorms, scorching heat, and lack of water, because he never, ever stopped moving.

It surprised even his commanding officers, who time and time again attempted to slow Rommel down. They preferred deliberation and discourse to advancement. It had a devastating effect on the momentum that Rommel had built with his troops—just as it does in our own lives.

So when you're frustrated in pursuit of your own goals, don't sit there and complain that you don't have what you want or that this obstacle won't budge. If you haven't even tried yet, then of course you will still be in the exact same place. You haven't actually pursued anything.

We talk a lot about courage as a society, but we forget that at its most basic level it's really just taking action—whether that's approaching someone you're intimidated by or deciding to finally crack a book on a subject you need to learn. Just as Earhart did, all the greats you admire started by saying, *Yes, let's go.* And they usually did it in less desirable circumstances than we'll ever suffer.

Just because the conditions aren't exactly to your liking, or you don't feel ready yet, doesn't mean you get a pass. If you want momentum, you'll have to create it yourself, right now, by getting up and getting started.

PRACTICE PERSISTENCE

> He says the best way out is always through
> And I agree to that, or in so far
> As I can see no way out but through.
>
> —ROBERT FROST

For nearly a year, General Ulysses S. Grant tried to crack the defenses of Vicksburg, a city perched high on the cliffs of the Mississippi, critical to the Confederacy's stranglehold on the most important river in the country. He tried attacking head-on. He tried to go around. He spent months digging a new canal that would change the course of the river. He blew the levees upstream and literally tried to float boats down into the city over flooded land.

None of it worked. All the while, the newspapers chattered. It'd been months without progress. Lincoln had sent a replacement, and the man was waiting in the wings. But Grant refused to be rattled, refused to rush or cease. He knew there was a weak spot somewhere. He'd find it or he'd make one.

His next move ran contrary to nearly all conventional military theory. He decided to run his boats past the gun batteries guarding the river—a considerable risk, because once down, they could not come back up. Despite an unprecedented nighttime firefight, nearly all the boats made the run unharmed. A few days later, Grant crossed the river about thirty miles downstream at the appropriately named Hard Times, Louisiana.

Grant's plan was bold: Leaving most of their supplies behind, his troops had to live off the land and make their way up the river, taking town after town along the way. By the time Grant laid siege to Vicksburg itself, the message to his men and his enemies was clear: He would never give up. The defenses would eventually crack. Grant was unstoppable. His victory wouldn't be pretty, but it was inexorable.

If we're to overcome our obstacles, this is the message to broadcast—internally and externally. We will not be stopped by failure, we will not be rushed or distracted by external noise. We will chisel and peg away at the obstacle until it is gone. Resistance is futile.

At Vicksburg, Grant learned two things. First, persistence and pertinacity were incredible assets and probably his main assets as a leader. Second, as often is the result from such dedication, in exhausting all the other traditional options, he'd been forced to try something new. That option— cutting loose from his supply trains and living off the spoils of hostile territory—was a previously untested strategy that the North could now use to slowly deplete the South of its resources and will to fight.

In persistence, he'd not only broken through: In trying it all the wrong ways, Grant discovered a totally new way—the way that would eventually win the war.

Grant's story is not the exception to the rule. It *is* the rule. This is how innovation works.

In 1878, Thomas Edison wasn't the only person experimenting with incandescent lights. But he was the only man willing to test six thousand different filaments—including one made from the beard hair of one of his men—inching closer each time to the one that would finally work.

And, of course, he eventually found it—proving that genius often really is just persistence in disguise. In applying the entirety of his physical and mental energy—in never growing weary or giving up—Edison had outlasted impatient competitors, investors, and the press to discover, in a piece of bamboo, of all things, the power to illuminate the world.

Nikola Tesla, who spent a frustrated year in Edison's lab during the invention of the lightbulb, once sneered that if Edison needed to find a needle in a haystack, he would "proceed at once" to simply "examine straw after straw until he found the object of his search." Well, sometimes that's exactly the right method.

As we butt up against obstacles, it is helpful to picture Grant and Edison. Grant with a cigar clenched in his mouth. Edison on his hands and knees in the laboratory for days straight. Both unceasing, embodying cool persistence and the spirit of the line from the Alfred Lord Tennyson poem about that other Ulysses, "to strive, to seek, to find." Both, refusing to give up. Turning over in their minds option after option, and trying each one with equal enthusiasm. Knowing that eventually—*inevitably*—one will work. Welcoming the opportunity to test and test and test, grateful for the priceless knowledge this reveals.

The thing standing in your way isn't going anywhere. You're not going to outthink it or outcreate it with some world-changing epiphany. You've got to look at it and the people around you, who have begun their inevitable chorus of doubts and excuses, and say, as Margaret Thatcher famously did: "You turn if you want to. The lady's not for turning."

Too many people think that great victories like Grant's and Edison's came from a flash of insight. That they cracked the problem with pure genius. In fact, it was the slow pressure, repeated from many different angles, the elimination of so many other more promising options, that slowly and surely churned the solution to the top of the pile. Their genius was unity of purpose, deafness to doubt, and the desire to stay at it.

So what if this method isn't as "scientific" or "proper" as others? The important part is that it works.

Working at it *works*. It's that simple. (But again, not easy.)

For most of what we attempt in life, chops are not the issue. We're usually skilled and knowledgeable and capable enough. But do we have the patience to refine our idea? The energy to beat on enough doors until we find investors or supporters? The persistence to slog through the politics and drama of working with a group?

Once you start attacking an obstacle, quitting is not an option. It cannot enter your head. Abandoning one path for another that might be more promising? Sure, but that's a far cry from giving up. Once you can envision yourself quitting altogether, you might as well ring the bell. It's done.

Consider this mind-set.

never in a hurry
never worried
never desperate
never stopping short

Remember and remind yourself of a phrase favored by Epictetus: "persist and resist." Persist in your efforts. Resist giving in to distraction, discouragement, or disorder.

There's no need to sweat this or feel rushed. No need to get upset or despair. You're not going anywhere—you're not going to be counted out. You're in this for the long haul.

Because when you play all the way to the whistle, there's no reason to worry about the clock. You know you won't stop until it's over—that every second available is yours to use. So temporary setbacks aren't discouraging. They are just bumps along a long road that you intend to travel all the way down.

Doing new things invariably means obstacles. A new path is, by definition, uncleared. Only with persistence and time can we cut away debris and remove impediments. Only in struggling with the impediments that made others quit can we find ourselves on untrodden territory—only by persisting and resisting can we learn what others were too impatient to be taught.

It's okay to be discouraged. It's not okay to quit. To know you want to quit but to plant your feet and keep inching closer until you take the impenetrable fortress you've decided to lay siege to in your own life—*that's* persistence.

Edison once explained that in inventing, "the first step is an intuition—and comes with a burst—*then* difficulties arise." What set Edison apart from other inventors is tolerance for these difficulties, and the steady dedication with which he applied himself toward solving them.

In other words: It's *supposed* to be hard. Your first attempts *aren't going to work*. It's goings to take a lot out of you—but energy is an asset we can always find more of. It's a renewable resource. Stop looking for an epiphany, and start looking for weak points. Stop looking for angels, and start looking for angles. There are options. Settle in for the long haul and then try each and every possibility, and you'll get there.

When people ask where we are, what we're doing, how that "situation" is coming along, the answer should be clear: We're working on it. We're getting closer. When setbacks come, we respond by working twice as hard.

ITERATE

What is defeat? Nothing but education; nothing but the
first steps to something better.

—WENDELL PHILLIPS

In Silicon Valley, start-ups don't launch with polished, finished businesses. Instead, they release their "Minimum
Viable Product" (MVP)—the most basic version of their core
idea with only one or two essential features.

The point is to immediately see how customers respond.
And, if that response is poor, to be able to fail cheaply and
quickly. To avoid making or investing in a product customers do not want.

As engineers now like to quip: Failure is a Feature.

But it's no joke. Failure really can be an asset if what
you're trying to do is improve, learn, or do something new.
It's the preceding feature of nearly all successes. There's
nothing shameful about being wrong, about changing
course. Each time it happens we have new options. Problems
become opportunities.

The old way of business—where companies guess what
customers want from research and then produce those
products in a lab, isolated and insulated from feedback—

reflects a fear of failure and is deeply fragile in relation to it. If the highly produced product flops on launch day, all that effort was wasted. If it succeeds, no one really knows why or what was responsible for that success. The MVP model, on the other hand, embraces failure and feedback. It gets stronger by failure, dropping the features that don't work, that customers don't find interesting, and then focusing the developers' limited resources on improving the features that do.

In a world where we increasingly work for ourselves, are responsible for ourselves, it makes sense to view ourselves like a start-up—a start-up of one.

And that means changing the relationship with failure. It means iterating, failing, and improving. Our capacity to try, try, try is inextricably linked with our ability and tolerance to fail, fail, fail.

On the path to successful action, we will fail—possibly many times. And that's okay. It can be a good thing, even. Action and failure are two sides of the same coin. One doesn't come without the other. What breaks this critical connection down is when people stop acting—because they've taken failure the wrong way.

When failure does come, ask: *What went wrong here? What can be improved? What am I missing?* This helps birth alternative ways of doing what needs to be done, ways that are often much better than what we started with. Failure puts you in corners you have to think your way out of. It is a source of breakthroughs.

This is why stories of great success are often preceded by epic failure—because the people in them went back to the drawing board. They weren't ashamed to fail, but spurred on, piqued by it. Sometimes in sports it takes a close loss to finally convince an underdog that they've got the ability to compete that competitor that had intimidated (and beat) them for so long. The loss might be painful, but as Franklin put it, it can also instruct.

With a business, we take most failures less personally and understand they're part of the process. If an investment or a new product pays off, great. If it fails, we're fine because we're prepared for it—we didn't invest every penny in that option.

Great entrepreneurs are:

never wedded to a position
never afraid to lose a little of their investment
never bitter or embarrassed
never out of the game for long

They slip many times, but they don't fall.

Even though we know that there are great lessons from failure—lessons we've seen with our own two eyes—we repeatedly shrink from it. We do everything we can to avoid it, thinking it's embarrassing or shameful. We fail, kicking and screaming.

Well why would I want to fail? It hurts.

I would never claim it doesn't. But can we acknowledge that anticipated, temporary failure certainly hurts less than catastrophic, permanent failure? Like any good school, learning from failure isn't free. The tuition is paid in discomfort or loss and having to start over.

Be glad to pay the cost. There will be no better teacher for your career, for your book, for your new venture. There's a saying about how the Irish ship captain located all the rocks in the harbor—using the bottom of his boat. Whatever works, right?

Remember Erwin Rommel and the quick work he made of the British and American forces in North Africa? There's another part to that story. The Allied forces actually chose that disadvantageous battlefield on purpose. Churchill knew that they would have to take their first stand against the Germans somewhere, but to do that *and* lose in Europe would be disastrous for morale.

In North Africa, the British learned how to fight the Germans—and early on they learned mostly by failure. But that was acceptable, because they'd anticipated a learning curve and planned for it. They welcomed it because they knew, like Grant and Edison did, what it meant: victory further down the road. As a result, the Allied troops Hitler faced in Italy were far better than those he'd faced in Africa and the ones he ultimately faced in France and Germany were better still.

The one way to guarantee we don't benefit from failure—to ensure it is a bad thing—is to not learn from it. To continue to try the same thing over and over (which is the definition of insanity for a reason). People fail in small ways all the time. But they don't learn. They don't listen. They don't see the problems that failure exposes. It doesn't make them better.

Thickheaded and resistant to change, these are the types who are too self-absorbed to realize that the world doesn't have time to plead, argue, and convince them of their errors. Soft bodied and hardheaded, they have too much armor and ego to fail well.

It's time you understand that the world is telling you something with each and every failure and action. It's feedback—giving you precise instructions on how to improve, it's trying to wake you up from your cluelessness. It's trying to teach you something. *Listen.*

Lessons come hard only if you're deaf to them. Don't be.

Being able to see and understand the world this way is part and parcel of overturning obstacles. Here, a negative becomes a positive. We turn what would otherwise be disappointment into opportunity. Failure shows us the way—by showing us what *isn't* the way.

FOLLOW THE PROCESS

> Under the comb
> the tangle and the straight path
> are the same.
>
> —HERACLITUS

Coach Nick Saban doesn't actually refer to it very often, but every one of his assistants and players lives by it. They say it for him, tattooing it at the front of their minds and on every action they take, because just two words are responsible for their unprecedented success: The Process.

Saban, the head coach of the University of Alabama football team—perhaps the most dominant dynasty in the history of college football—doesn't focus on what every other coach focuses on, or at least not the *way* they do. He teaches The Process.

> *"Don't think about winning the SEC Championship. Don't think about the national championship. Think about what you needed to do in this drill, on this play, in this moment. That's the process: Let's think about what we can do today, the task at hand."*

In the chaos of sport, as in life, process provides us a way.

It says: Okay, you've got to do something very difficult. Don't focus on that. Instead break it down into pieces. Simply do what you *need* to do *right now*. And do it well. And then move on to the next thing. Follow the process and not the prize.

The road to back-to-back championships is just that, a road. And you travel along a road in steps. Excellence is a matter of steps. Excelling at this one, then that one, and then the one after that. Saban's process is exclusively this— existing in the present, taking it one step at a time, not getting distracted by anything else. Not the other team, not the scoreboard or the crowd.

The process is about finishing. Finishing games. Finishing workouts. Finishing film sessions. Finishing drives. Finishing reps. Finishing plays. Finishing blocks. Finishing the smallest task you have right in front of you and finishing it well.

Whether it's pursuing the pinnacle of success in your field or simply surviving some awful or trying ordeal, the same approach works. Don't think about the end—think about surviving. Making it from meal to meal, break to break, checkpoint to checkpoint, paycheck to paycheck, one day at a time.

And when you really get it right, even the hardest things become manageable. Because the process is relaxing. Under its influence, we needn't panic. Even mammoth tasks become just a series of component parts.

This was what the great nineteenth-century pioneer of meteorology, James Pollard Espy, was shown in a chance encounter as a young man. Unable to read and write until he was eighteen, Espy attended a rousing speech by the famous orator Henry Clay. After the talk, a spellbound Espy tried to make his way toward Clay, but he couldn't form the words to speak to his idol. One of his friends shouted out for him: "He wants to be like you, even though he can't read."

Clay grabbed one of his posters, which had the word CLAY written in big letters. He looked at Espy and said, "You see that, boy?" pointing to a letter. "That's an A. Now, you've only got twenty-five more letters to go."

Espy had just been gifted the process. Within a year, he started college.

I know that seems almost too simple. But envision, for a second, a master practicing an exceedingly difficult craft and making it look effortless. There's no strain, no struggling. So relaxed. No exertion or worry. Just one clean movement after another. That's a result of the process.

We can channel this, too. We needn't scramble like we're so often inclined to do when some difficult task sits in front of us. Remember the first time you saw a complicated algebra equation? It was a jumble of symbols and unknowns. But then you stopped, took a deep breath, and broke it down. You isolated the variables, solved for them, and all that was left was the answer.

Do that now, for whatever obstacles you come across. We can take a breath, do the immediate, composite part in front of us—and follow its thread into the next action. Everything in order, everything connected.

When it comes to our actions, disorder and distraction are death. The unordered mind loses track of what's in front of it—what matters—and gets distracted by thoughts of the future. The process is order, it keeps our perceptions in check and our actions in sync.

It seems obvious, but we forget this when it matters most.

Right now, if I knocked you down and pinned you to the ground, how would you respond? You'd probably panic. And then you'd push with all your strength to get me off you. It wouldn't work; just using my body weight, I would be able to keep your shoulders against the ground with little effort—and you'd grow exhausted fighting it.

That's the opposite of the process.

There is a much easier way. First, you don't panic, you conserve your energy. You don't do anything stupid like get yourself choked out by acting without thinking. You focus on not letting it get worse. Then you get your arms up, to brace and create some breathing room, some space. Now work to get on your side. From there you can start to break down my hold on you: Grab an arm, trap a leg, buck with your hips, slide in a knee and push away.

It'll take some time, but you'll get yourself out. At each step, the person on top is forced to give a little up, until there's nothing left. Then you're free—thanks to the process.

Being trapped is just a position, not a fate. You get out of it by addressing and eliminating each part of that position through small, deliberate actions—not by trying (and failing) to push it away with superhuman strength.

With our business rivals, we rack our brains to think of some mind-blowing new product that will make them irrelevant, and, in the process, we take our eye off the ball. We shy away from writing a book or making a film even though it's our dream because it's so much work—we can't imagine how we get from here to there.

How often do we compromise or settle because we feel that the real solution is too ambitious or outside our grasp?

How often do we assume that change is impossible because it's too big? Involves too many different groups? Or worse, how many people are paralyzed by all their ideas and inspirations? They chase them all and go nowhere, distracting themselves and never making headway. They're brilliant, sure, but they rarely execute. They rarely get where they want and need to go.

All these issues are solvable. Each would collapse beneath the process. We've just wrongly assumed that it has to happen all at once, and we give up at the thought of it. We are A-to-Z thinkers, fretting about A, obsessing over Z, yet forgetting all about B through Y.

We want to have goals, yes, so everything we do can be in the service of something purposeful. When we know what we're really setting out to do, the obstacles that arise tend to seem smaller, more manageable. When we don't, each one looms larger and seems impossible. Goals help put the blips and bumps in proper proportion.

When we get distracted, when we start caring about something other than our own progress and efforts, the process is the helpful, if occasionally bossy, voice in our head. It is the bark of the wise, older leader who knows exactly who he is and what he's got to do: *Shut up. Go back to your stations and try to think about what we are going to do ourselves instead of worrying about what's going on out there. You know what your job is. Stop jawing and get to work.*

The process is the voice that demands we take responsibility and ownership. That prompts us to *act* even if only in a small way.

Like a relentless machine, subjugating resistance each and every way it exists, little by little. Moving forward, one step at a time. Subordinate strength to the process. Replace fear with the process. Depend on it. Lean on it. Trust in it.

Take your time, don't rush. Some problems are harder than others. Deal with the ones right in front of you first. Come back to the others later. You'll get there.

The process is about doing the right things, *right now*. Not worrying about what might happen later, or the results, or the whole picture.

DO YOUR JOB, DO IT RIGHT

Whatever is rightly done, however humble, is noble. (*Quidvis recte factum quamvis humile praeclarum.*)

—SIR HENRY ROYCE

Long past his humble beginnings, President Andrew Johnson would speak proudly of his career as a tailor before he entered politics. "My garments never ripped or gave way," he would say.

On the campaign trail, a heckler once tried to embarrass him by shouting about his working-class credentials. Johnson replied without breaking stride: "That does not disconcert me in the least; for when I used to be a tailor I had the reputation of being a good one, and making close fits, always punctual with my customers, and always did good work."

Another president, James Garfield, paid his way through college in 1851 by persuading his school, the Western Reserve Eclectic Institute, to let him be the janitor in exchange for tuition. He did the job every day smiling and without a hint of shame. Each morning, he'd ring the university's bell tower to start the classes—his day already having long begun—and stomp to class with cheer and eagerness.

Within just one year of starting at the school he was a professor—teaching a full course load in addition to his studies. By his twenty-sixth birthday he was the dean.

This is what happens when you do your job—whatever it is—and do it well.

These men went from humble poverty to power by always doing what they were asked to do—and doing it right and with real pride. And doing it better than anyone else. In fact, doing it well because no one else wanted to do it.

Sometimes, on the road to where we are going or where we want to be, we have to do things that we'd rather not do. Often when we are just starting out, our first jobs "introduce us to the broom," as Andrew Carnegie famously put it. There's nothing shameful about sweeping. It's just another opportunity to excel—and to learn.

But you, you're so busy thinking about the future, you don't take any pride in the tasks you're given right now. You just phone it all in, cash your paycheck, and dream of some higher station in life. Or you think, *This is just a job, it isn't who I am, it doesn't matter.*

Foolishness.

Everything we do matters—whether it's making smoothies while you save up money or studying for the bar—even after you already achieved the success you sought. Everything is a chance to do and be your best. Only self-absorbed assholes think they are too good for whatever their current station requires.

Wherever we are, whatever we're doing and wherever we are going, we owe it to ourselves, to our art, to the world to do it well. That's our primary duty. And our obligation. When action is our priority, vanity falls away.

An artist is given many different canvases and commissions in their lifetime, and what matters is that they treat each one as a priority. Whether it's the most glamorous or highest paying is irrelevant. Each project matters, and the only degrading part is giving less than one is capable of giving.

Same goes for us. We will be and do many things in our lives. Some are prestigious, some are onerous, none are beneath us. To whatever we face, our job is to respond with:

hard work
honesty
helping others as best we can

You should never have to ask yourself, *But what am I supposed to do now?* Because you know the answer: your job.

Whether anyone notices, whether we're paid for it, whether the project turns out successfully—it doesn't matter. We can and always should act with those three traits—no matter the obstacle.

There will never be any obstacles that can ever truly prevent us from carrying out our obligation—harder or easier challenges, sure, but never impossible. Each and every task requires our best. Whether we're facing down bankruptcy and angry customers, or raking in money and deciding how to grow from here, if we do our best we can be proud of our choices and confident they're the right ones. Because we did our job—whatever it is.

Yeah, yeah, I get it. "Obligations" sound stuffy and oppressive. You want to be able to do whatever you want.

But duty is beautiful, and inspiring and empowering.

Steve Jobs cared even about the inside of his products, making sure they were beautifully designed even though the users would never see them. Taught by his father—who finished even the back of his cabinets though they would be hidden against the wall—to think like a craftsman. In every design predicament, Jobs knew his marching orders: Respect the craft and make something beautiful.

Every situation is different, obviously. We're not inventing the next iPad or iPhone, but we are making something for someone—even if it's just our own résumé. Every part—especially the work that nobody sees, the tough things we wanted to avoid or could have skated away from—we can treat same way Jobs did: with pride and dedication.

The great psychologist Viktor Frankl, survivor of three concentration camps, found presumptuousness in the age-old question: "What is the meaning of life?" As though it is someone else's responsibility to tell you. Instead, he said, the world is asking *you* that question. And it's your job to answer with your actions.

In every situation, life is asking us a question, and our actions are the answer. Our job is simply to answer well.

Right action—unselfish, dedicated, masterful, creative—that is the answer to that question. That's one way to find the meaning of life. And how to turn every obstacle into an opportunity.

If you see any of this as a burden, you're looking at it the wrong way.

Because all we need to do is those three little duties—to try hard, to be honest, and to help others and ourselves. That's all that's been asked of us. No more and no less.

Sure, the goal is important. But never forget that each individual instance matters, too—each is a snapshot of the whole. The whole isn't certain, only the instances are.

How you do anything is how you can do everything.

We can always act right.

WHAT'S RIGHT IS WHAT WORKS

The cucumber is bitter? Then throw it out.
There are brambles in the path? Then go around.
That's all you need to know.

—MARCUS AURELIUS

In 1915, deep in the jungles of South America, the rising conflict between two rival American fruit companies came to a head. Each desperately wanted to acquire the same five thousand acres of valuable land.

The issue? Two different locals claimed to own the deed to the plantation. In the no-man's-land between Honduras and Guatemala, neither company was able to tell who was the rightful owner so they could buy it from them.

How they each responded to this problem was defined by their company's organization and ethos. One company was big and powerful, the other crafty and cunning. The first, one of the most powerful corporations in the United States: United Fruit. The second, a small upstart owned by Samuel Zemurray.

To solve the problem, United Fruit dispatched a team of high-powered lawyers. They set out in search of every file and scrap of paper in the country, ready to pay whatever it cost to win. Money, time, and resources were no object.

Zemurray, the tiny, uneducated competitor, was outmatched, right? He couldn't play their game. So he didn't. Flexible, fluid, and defiant, he just met separately with both of the supposed owners and bought the land from each of them. He paid twice, sure, but it was *over*. The land was his. Forget the rule book, settle the issue.

This is *pragmatism* embodied. Don't worry about the "right" way, worry about the *right* way. This is how we get things done.

Zemurray always treated obstacles this way. Told he couldn't build a bridge he needed across the Utila River—because government officials had been bribed by competitors to make bridges illegal—Zemurray had his engineers build two long piers instead. And in between which reached out far into the center of the river, they strung a temporary pontoon that could be assembled and deployed to connect them in a matter of hours. Railroads ran down each side of the riverbank, going in opposite direction. When United Fruit complained, Zemurray laughed and replied: "Why, that's no bridge. It's just a couple of little old wharfs."

Sometimes you do it *this* way. Sometimes *that* way. Not deploying the tactics you learned in school but adapting them to fit each and every situation. Any way that *works*—that's the motto.

We spend a lot of time thinking about how things are supposed to be, or what the rules say we should do. Trying to get it all perfect. We tell ourselves that we'll get started once the conditions are right, or once we're sure we can trust this or that. When, really, it'd be better to focus on making due with what we've got. On focusing on results instead of pretty methods.

As they say in Brazilian jujitsu, it doesn't matter how you get your opponents to the ground, after all, only that you take them down.

What Zemurray never lost sight of was the mission: getting bananas across the river. Whether it was a bridge or two piers with a dock in the middle, it didn't matter so long as it got the cargo where it needed to go. When he wanted to plant bananas on a particular plantation, it wasn't important to find the rightful owner of the land—it was to *become* the rightful owner.

You've got your mission, whatever it is. To accomplish it, like the rest of us you're in the pinch between the way you wish things were and the way they actually are (which always seem to be a disaster). How far are you willing to go? What are you willing to do about it?

Scratch the complaining. No waffling. No submitting to powerlessness or fear. You can't just run home to Mommy. How are you going to solve this problem? How are you going to get around the rules that hold you back?

Maybe you'll need to be a little more cunning or conniving than feels comfortable. Sometimes that requires ignoring some outdated regulations or asking for forgiveness from management later rather than for permission (which would be denied) right now. But if you've got an important mission, all that matters is that you accomplish it.

At twenty-one, Richard Wright was not the world-famous author he would eventually be. But poor and black, he decided he would read and no one could stop him. Did he storm the library and make a scene? No, not in the Jim Crow South he didn't. Instead, he forged a note that said, "Dear Madam: Will you please let this nigger boy have some books by HL Mencken?" (because no one would write that about themselves, right?), and checked them out with a stolen library card, pretending they were for someone else.

With the stakes this high, you better be willing to bend the rules or do something desperate or crazy. To thumb your nose at the authorities and say: *What? This is not a bridge. I don't know what you're talking about.* Or, in some cases, giving the middle finger to the people trying to hold you down and blowing right through their evil, disgusting rules.

Pragmatism is not so much realism as flexibility. There are a lot of ways to get from point A to point B. It doesn't have to be a straight line. It's just got to get you where you need to go. But so many of us spend so much time looking for the perfect solution that we pass up what's right in front of us.

As Deng Xiaoping once said, "I don't care if the cat is black or white, so long as it catches mice."

The Stoics had their own reminder: "Don't go expecting Plato's Republic."

Because you're never going to find that kind of perfection. Instead, do the best with what you've got. Not that pragmatism is inherently at odds with idealism or pushing the ball forward. The first iPhone was revolutionary, but it still shipped without a copy-and-paste feature or a handful of other features Apple would have liked to have included. Steve Jobs, the supposed perfectionist, knew that at some point, you have to compromise. What mattered was that you got it done and it *worked*.

Start thinking like a radical pragmatist: still ambitious, aggressive, and rooted in ideals, but also imminently practical and guided by the possible. Not on everything you would like to have, not on changing the world right at this moment, but ambitious enough to get everything you *need*. Don't think small, but make the distinction between the critical and the extra.

Think progress, not perfection.

Under this kind of force, obstacles break apart. They have no choice. Since you're going around them or making them irrelevant, there is nothing for them to resist.

IN PRAISE OF THE FLANK ATTACK

Whoever cannot seek
the unforeseen sees nothing,
for the known way
is an impasse.

—HERACLITUS

The popular image of George Washington in American lore is of a brave and bold general, towering over everything he surveyed, repelling the occupied and tyrannical British. Of course, the true picture is a little less glorious. Washington wasn't a guerrilla, but he was close enough. He was wily, evasive, often refusing to battle.

His army was small, undertrained, undersupplied, and fragile. He waged a war mostly of defense, deliberately avoiding large formations of British troops. For all the rhetoric, most of his maneuvers were pinpricks against a stronger, bigger enemy. Hit and run. Stick and move.

Never attack where it is obvious, Washington told his men. Don't attack as the enemy would expect, he explained, instead, "Where little danger is apprehended, the more the enemy will be unprepared and consequently there is the fairest prospect of success." He had a powerful sense of which minor skirmishes would feel and look like major victories.

His most glorious "victory" wasn't even a direct battle with the British. Instead, Washington, nearly at the end of his rope, crossed the Delaware at dawn on Christmas Day to attack a group of sleeping German mercenaries who may or may not have been drunk.

He was actually better at withdrawing than at advancing—skilled at saving troops that otherwise would have been lost in defeat. Washington rarely got trapped—he always had a way out. Hoping simply to tire out his enemy, this evasiveness was a powerful weapon—though not necessarily a glamorous one.

It's not surprising then, as the general of the Continental Army and the country's first president, that his legacy has been whitewashed and embellished a little. And he's not the only general we've done it for. The great myth of history, propagated by movies and stories and our own ignorance, is that wars are won and lost by two great armies going head-to-head in battle. It's a dramatic, courageous notion—but also very, very wrong.

In a study of some 30 conflicts comprising more than 280 campaigns from ancient to modern history, the brilliant strategist and historian B. H. Liddell Hart came to a stunning conclusion: In only 6 of the 280 campaigns was the decisive victory a result of a direct attack on the enemy's main army.

Only six. That's 2 percent.

If not from pitched battles, where do we find victory?

From everywhere else. From the flanks. From the unexpected. From the psychological. From drawing opponents out from their defenses. From the untraditional. From anything *but* . . .

As Hart writes in his masterwork *Strategy*:

> [T]he Great Captain will take even the most hazardous indirect approach—if necessary over mountains, deserts or swamps, with only a fraction of the forces, even cutting himself loose from his communications. Facing, in fact, every unfavorable condition rather than accept the risk of stalemate invited by direct approach.

When you're at your wit's end, straining and straining with all your might, when people tell you you look like you might pop a vein . . .

Take a step back, then go around the problem. Find some leverage. Approach from what is called the "line of least expectation."

What's your first instinct when faced with a challenge? Is it to outspend the competition? Argue with people in an attempt to change long-held opinions? Are you trying to barge through the front door? Because the back door, side doors, and windows may have been left wide open.

Whatever you're doing, it's going to be harder (to say nothing of impossible) if your plan includes defying physics or logic. Instead, think of Grant realizing he had to bypass Vicksburg—not go at it—in order to capture it. Think of Hall of Fame coach Phil Jackson and his famous triangle offense, which is designed to automatically route the basketball *away* from defensive pressure rather than attack it directly.

If we're starting from scratch and the established players have had time to build up their defenses, there is just no way we are going to beat them on their strengths. So it's smarter to not even try, but instead focus our limited resources elsewhere.

Part of the reason why a certain skill often seems so effortless for great masters is not just because they've mastered the process—they really are doing less than the rest of us who don't know any better. They choose to exert only calculated force where it will be effective, rather than straining and struggling with pointless attrition tactics.

As someone once put it after fighting Jigoro Kano, the legendary five-foot-tall founder of judo, "Trying to fight with Kano was like trying to fight with an empty jacket!"

That can be you.

Being outnumbered, coming from behind, being low on funds, these don't have to be disadvantages. They can be gifts. Assets that make us less likely to commit suicide with a head-to-head attack. These things *force* us to be creative, to find workarounds, to sublimate the ego and do anything to win besides challenging our enemies where they are strongest. These are the signs that tell us to approach from an oblique angle.

In fact, having the advantage of size or strength or power is often the birthing ground for true and fatal weakness. The inertia of success makes it much harder to truly develop good technique. People or companies who have that size advantage never really have to learn the process when they've been able to coast on brute force. And that works for them . . . until it doesn't. Until they meet you and you make quick work of them with deft and oblique maneuvers, when you refuse to face them in the one setting they know: head-to-head.

We're in the game of little defeating big. Therefore, Force can't try to match Force.

Of course, when pushed, the natural instinct is always to push back. But martial arts teach us that we have to ignore this impulse. We can't push back, we have to *pull* until opponents lose their balance. Then we make our move.

The art of the side-door strategy is a vast, creative space. And it is by no means limited to war, business, or sales.

The great philosopher Søren Kierkegaard rarely sought to convince people directly from a position of authority. Instead of lecturing, he practiced a method he called "indirect communication." Kierkegaard would write under pseudonyms, where each fake personality would embody a different platform or perspective—writing multiple times on the same subject from multiple angles to convey his point emotionally and dramatically. He would rarely tell the reader "do this" or "think that." Instead he would *show* new ways of looking at or understanding the world.

You don't convince people by challenging their longest and most firmly held opinions. You find common ground and work from there. Or you look for leverage to make them listen. Or you create an alterative with so much support from other people that the opposition voluntarily abandons its views and joins your camp.

The way that works isn't always the most impressive. Sometimes it even feels like you're taking a shortcut or fighting unfairly. There's a lot of pressure to try to match people move for move, as if sticking with what works for you is somehow cheating. Let me save you the guilt and self-flagellation: It's not.

You're acting like a real strategist. You aren't just throwing your weight around and hoping it works. You're not wasting your energy in battles driven by ego and pride rather than tactical advantage.

Believe it or not, *this* is the hard way. That's why it works.

Remember, sometimes the longest way around is the shortest way home.

USE OBSTACLES AGAINST
THEMSELVES

Wise men are able to make a fitting use even
of their enmities.

—PLUTARCH

Gandhi didn't fight for independence for India. The British Empire did all of the fighting—and, as it happens, all of the losing.

That was deliberate, of course. Gandhi's extensive satyagraha campaign and civil disobedience show that *action* has many definitions. It's not always moving forward or even obliquely. It can also be a matter of positions. It can be a matter of taking a stand.

Sometimes you overcome obstacles not by attacking them but by withdrawing and letting them attack you. You can use the actions of others against themselves instead of acting yourself.

Weak compared to the forces he hoped to change, Gandhi leaned into that weakness, exaggerated it, exposed himself. He said to the most powerful occupying military in the world, *I'm marching to the ocean to collect salt in direct violation of your laws.* He was provoking them—*What are you going to do about it? There is nothing wrong with what we're doing*—knowing that it placed authorities in an impossible dilemma: Enforce a bankrupt policy or abdicate. Within that framework, the military's enormous strength is neutralized. Its very usage is counterproductive.

Martin Luther King Jr., taking Gandhi's lead, told his followers that they would meet "physical force with soul force." In other words, they would use the power of opposites. In the face of violence they would be peaceful, to hate they would answer with love—and in the process, they would expose those attributes as indefensible and evil.

Opposites work. Nonaction can be action. It uses the power of others and allows us to absorb their power as our own. Letting them—or the obstacle—do the work for us.

Just ask the Russians, who defeated Napoléon and the Nazis not by rigidly protecting their borders but by retreating into the interior and leaving the winter to do their work on the enemy, bogged down in battles far from home.

Is this an action? You bet it is.

Perhaps your enemy or obstacle really is insurmountable—as it was for many of these groups. Perhaps in this case, you haven't got the ability to win through attrition (persistence) or you don't want to risk learning on the job (iterate). Okay. You're still a long way from needing to give up.

It is, however, time to acknowledge that some adversity might be impossible for you to defeat—no matter how hard you try. Instead, you must find some way to use the adversity, its *energy*, to help yourself.

Before the invention of steam power, boat captains had an ingenious way of defeating the wickedly strong current of the Mississippi River. A boat going upriver would pull alongside a boat about to head downriver, and after wrapping a rope around a tree or a rock, the boats would tie themselves to each other. The second boat would let go and let the river take it downstream, slingshotting the other vessel upstream.

So instead of fighting obstacles, find a means of *making them defeat themselves.*

There is a famous story of Alexander the Great doing just that—and it was Alexander's masterful use of an obstacle against itself that gave observers their first hint that the ambitious teenager might one day conquer the world. As a young man, he trained his famous horse Bucephalus—the horse that even his father, King Philip II of Macedon, could not break—by tiring him out. While others had tried sheer force and whips and ropes, only to be bucked off, Alexander succeeded by lightly mounting and simply hanging on until the horse was calm. Having exhausted himself, Bucephalus had no choice but to submit to his rider's influence. Alexander would ride into battle on this faithful horse for the next twenty years.

Now what of your obstacles?

Yes, sometimes we need to learn from Amelia Earhart and just take action. But we also have to be ready to see that *restraint* might be the best action for us to take. Sometimes in your life you need to have patience—wait for temporary obstacles to fizzle out. Let two jousting egos sort themselves out instead of jumping immediately into the fray. Sometimes a problem needs *less* of you—fewer people period—and not more.

When we want things too badly we can be our own worst enemy. In our eagerness, we strip the very screw we want to turn and make it impossible to ever get what we want. We spin our tires in the snow or mud and dig a deeper rut—one that we'll never get out of.

We get so consumed with moving forward that we forget that there are other ways to get where we are heading. It doesn't naturally occur to us that standing still—or in some cases, even going backward—might be the best way to advance. Don't just do something, stand there!

We push and push—to get a raise, a new client, to prevent some exigency from happening. In fact, the best way to get what we want might be to reexamine those desires in the first place. Or it might be to aim for something else entirely, and use the impediment as an opportunity to explore a new direction. In doing so, we might end up creating a new venture that replaces our insufficient income entirely. Or we might discover that in ignoring clients, we attract more—finding that they want to work with someone who does not so badly want to work with them. Or we rethink that disaster we feared (along with everyone else) and come up with a way to profit from it when and if it happens.

We wrongly assume that moving forward is the only way to progress, the only way we can win. Sometimes, staying put, going sideways, or moving backward is actually the best way to eliminate what blocks or impedes your path.

There is a certain humility required in the approach. It means accepting that the way you originally wanted to do things is not possible. You just haven't got it in you to do it the "traditional" way. But so what?

What matters is whether a certain approach gets you to where you want to go. And let's be clear, using obstacles against themselves is very different from doing nothing. Passive resistance is, in fact, incredibly active. But those actions come in the form of discipline, self-control, fearlessness, determination, and grand strategy.

The great strategist Saul Alinsky believed that if you "push a negative hard enough and deep enough it will break through into its counterside." Every positive has its negative. Every negative has its positive. The *action* is in the pushing through—all the way through to the other side. *Making* a negative into a positive.

This should be great solace. It means that very few obstacles are ever too big for us. Because that bigness might in fact be an advantage. Because we can use that bigness against the obstacle itself. Remember, a castle can be an intimidating, impenetrable fortress, or it can be turned into a prison when surrounded. The difference is simply a shift in action and approach.

We can use the things that block us to our advantage, letting them do the difficult work for us. Sometimes this means leaving the obstacle as is, instead of trying so hard to change it.

The harder Bucephalus ran, the sooner he got tired out. The more vicious the police response to civil disobedience, the more sympathetic the cause becomes. The more they fight, the easier it becomes. The harder you fight, the less you'll achieve (other than exhaustion).

So it goes with our problems.

CHANNEL YOUR ENERGY

—————

> When jarred, unavoidably, by circumstance revert at once
> to yourself and don't lose the rhythm more than you can help.
> You'll have a better grasp of harmony if you keep going
> back to it.

—MARCUS AURELIUS

As a tennis player, Arthur Ashe was a beautiful contradiction. To survive segregation in the 1950s and 1960s, he learned from his father to mask his emotions and feelings on the court. No reacting, no getting upset at missed shots, and no challenging bad calls. Certainly, as a black player he could not afford to show off, celebrate, or be seen as trying too hard.

But his actual form and playing style was something quite different. All the energy and emotion he had to suppress was channeled into a bold and graceful playing form. While his face was controlled, his body was alive—fluid, brilliant, and all over the court. His style is best described in the epithet he created for himself: "physically loose and mentally tight."

For Arthur Ashe, this combination created a nearly un-beatable tennis game. As a person he'd control his emotions, but as a player he was swashbuckling, bold, and cool. He dove for balls and took—and made—the kind of shots that made other players gasp. He was able to do this because he was free. He was free where it mattered: inside.

Other players, free to celebrate, free to throw tantrums or glower at refs and opponents, never seemed to be able to handle the pressure of high-stakes matches the way Ashe could. They often mistook Ashe as inhuman, as bottled up. Feelings need an outlet, of course, but Ashe deployed them to fuel his explosive speed, in his slams and chips and dives. In the abandon with which he played, there was none of the quiet prudence with which he composed himself.

Adversity can harden you. Or it can loosen you up and make you better—if you let it.

Rename it and claim it, that's what Ashe did—as have many other black athletes. The boxer Joe Louis, for example, knew that racist white boxing fans would not tolerate an emotional black fighter, so he sublimated all displays behind a steely, blank face. Known as the Ring Robot, he greatly intimidated opponents by seeming almost inhuman. He took a disadvantage and turned it into an unexpected asset in the ring.

We all have our own constraints to deal with—rules and social norms we're required to observe that we'd rather not. Dress codes, protocols, procedures, legal obligations, and company hierarchies that are all telling us how we have to behave. Think about it too much and it can start to feel oppressive, even suffocating. If we're not careful, this is likely to throw us off our game.

Instead of giving in to frustration, we can put it to good use. It can power our actions, which, unlike our disposition, become stronger and better when loose and bold. While others obsess with observing the rules, we're subtly undermining them and subverting them to our advantage. Think water. When dammed by a man-made obstacle, it does not simply sit stagnant. Instead, its energy is stored and deployed, fueling the power plants that run entire cities.

Toussaint Louverture, the former Haitian slave turned general, so exasperated his French enemies that they once remarked: *"Cet homme fait donc l'ouverture partout"* ("This man makes an opening everywhere"). He was so fluid, so uncontainable, he was actually given the surname Louverture, meaning "the opening." It makes sense. Everything in his life had been an obstacle, and he turned as many of his experiences as he could into openings. Why should troops or politics or mountains or Napoléon himself have been any different?

And yet we feel like going to pieces when the PowerPoint projector won't work (instead of throwing it aside and delivering an exciting talk without notes). We stir up gossip with our coworkers (instead of pounding something productive out on our keyboards). We act out, instead of *act*.

But think of an athlete "in the pocket," "in the zone," "on a streak," and the seemingly insurmountable obstacles that fall in the face of that effortless state. Enormous deficits collapse, every pass or shot hits its intended target, fatigue melts away. Those athletes might be stopped from carrying out this or that action, but not from their goal. External factors influence the path, but not the direction: forward.

What setbacks in our lives could resist that elegant, fluid, and powerful mastery?

To be physically and mentally loose takes no talent. That's just recklessness. (We want right action, not action *period*.)

To be physically and mentally tight? That's called anxiety. It doesn't work, either. Eventually we snap. But physical looseness combined with mental restraint? That is powerful.

It's a power that drives our opponents and competitors nuts. They think we're toying with them. It's maddening—like we aren't even trying, like we've tuned out the world. Like we're immune to external stressors and limitations on the march toward our goals.

Because we are.

SEIZE THE OFFENSIVE

> The best men are not those who have waited for chances
> but who have taken them; besieged chance, conquered the
> chance, and made chance the servitor.
>
> —E. H. CHAPIN

In the spring of 2008, Barack Obama's presidential candidacy was imperiled. A race scandal involving inflammatory remarks by his pastor, Reverend Jeremiah Wright, threatened to unravel his campaign—to break the thin bond he'd established between black and white voters at a critical moment in the primaries.

Race, religion, demographics, controversy emulsified into one. It was the kind of political disaster that political campaigns do not survive, leaving most candidates so paralyzed by fear that they defer taking action. Their typical response is to hide, ignore, obfuscate, or distance themselves.

Whatever one thinks about Obama's politics, no one can deny what happened next. He turned one of the lowest moments in his campaign into a surprise offensive.

Against all advice and convention, he decided that he would take action and that this negative situation was actually a "teachable moment." Obama channeled the attention and energy swirling around the controversy to draw a national audience and speak directly to the American people of the divisive issue of race.

This speech, known today as the "A More Perfect Union" speech, was a transformative moment. Instead of distancing himself, Obama addressed everything directly. In doing so, he not only neutralized a potentially fatal controversy but created an opportunity to seize the electoral high ground. Absorbing the power of that negative situation, his campaign was instantly infused with an energy that propelled it into the White House.

If you think it's simply enough to take advantage of the opportunities that arise in your life, you will fall short of greatness. Anyone sentient can do that. What you must do is learn how to press forward precisely when everyone around you sees disaster.

It's at the seemingly bad moments, when people least expect it, that we can act swiftly and unexpectedly to pull off a big victory. While others are arrested by discouragement, we are not. We see the moment differently, and act accordingly.

Ignore the politics and focus on the brilliant strategic advice that Obama's adviser Rahm Emanuel, once gave him. "You never want a serious crisis to go to waste. Things that we had postponed for too long, that were long-term, are now immediate and must be dealt with. [A] crisis provides the opportunity for us to do things that you could not do before."

If you look at history, some of our greatest leaders used shocking or negative events to push through much-needed reforms that otherwise would have had little chance of passing. We can apply that in our own lives.

You always planned to do something. Write a screenplay. Travel. Start a business. Approach a possible mentor. Launch a movement.

Well, now something has happened—some disruptive event like a failure or an accident or a tragedy. *Use it.*

Perhaps you're stuck in bed recovering. Well, now you have time to write. Perhaps your emotions are overwhelming and painful, turn it into material. You lost your job or a relationship? That's awful, but now you can travel unencumbered. You're having a problem? Now you know exactly what to approach that mentor about. Seize this moment to deploy the plan that has long sat dormant in your head. Every chemical reaction requires a catalyst. Let this be yours.

Ordinary people shy away from negative situations, just as they do with failure. They do their best to avoid trouble. What great people do is the opposite. They are their best in these situations. They turn personal tragedy or misfortune— really anything, everything—to their advantage.

But this crisis in front of you? You're wasting it feeling sorry for yourself, feeling tired or disappointed. You forget: Life speeds on the bold and favors the brave.

We sit here and complain that we're not being given opportunities or chances. But we are.

At certain moments in our brief existences we are faced with great trials. Often those trials are frustrating, unfortunate, or unfair. They seem to come exactly when we think we need them the least. The question is: Do we accept this as an exclusively negative event, or can we get past whatever negativity or adversity it represents and mount an offensive? Or more precisely, can we see that this "problem" presents an opportunity for a solution that we have long been waiting for?

If you don't *take* that, it's on you.

Napoleon described war in simple terms: Two armies are two bodies that clash and attempt to frighten each other. At impact, there is a moment of panic and it is *that moment* that the superior commander turns to his advantage.

Rommel, for instance, was renowned for his *Fronter-führing*, his sixth sense for the decisive point in battle. He had an acute ability to feel—even in the heat of the moment—the precise instance when going on the offensive would be most effective. It's what allowed him to, repeatedly and often unbelievably, snatch victory from the jaws of defeat.

Where others saw disaster or, at best, simply the normal noise and dust of a battle, Rommel sensed opportunities. "It is given to me," he said, "to feel where the enemy is weak." And on these feelings he would attack with every iota of his energy. Seizing control of the tempo and never giving it up.

Great commanders look for decision points. For it is bursts of energy directed at decisive points that break things wide open. They press and press and press and then, exactly when the situation seems hopeless—or, more likely, hopelessly deadlocked—they press once more.

In many battles, as in life, the two opposing forces will often reach a point of mutual exhaustion. It's the one who rises the next morning after a long day of fighting and rallies, instead of retreating—the one who says, *I intend to attack and whip them right here and now*—who will carry victory home . . . intelligently.

This is what Obama did. Not shirking, not giving in to exhaustion despite the long neck-and-neck primary. But rallying at the last moment. Transcending the challenge and reframing it, triumphing as a result of it. He turned an ugly incident into that "teachable moment," and one of the most profound speeches on race in our history.

The obstacle is not only turned upside down but used as a catapult.

PREPARE FOR
NONE OF IT TO WORK

In the meantime, cling tooth and nail to the following rule:
not to give in to adversity, not to trust prosperity, and always
take full note of fortune's habit of behaving just as she
pleases.

—SENECA

Perceptions can be managed. Actions can be directed.
We can always think clearly, respond creatively. Look
for opportunity, seize the initiative.

What we can't do is control the world around us—not as
much as we'd like to, anyway. We might perceive things well,
then act rightly, and fail anyway.

Run it through your head like this: Nothing can ever prevent us from trying. Ever.

All creativity and dedication aside, after we've tried, *some*
obstacles may turn out to be impossible to overcome. Some
actions are rendered impossible, some paths impassable.
Some things are bigger than us.

This is not necessarily a bad thing. Because we can turn that
obstacle upside down, too, simply by using it as an opportunity
to practice some other virtue or skill—even if it is just learning
to accept that bad things happen, or practicing humility.

It's an infinitely elastic formula: In every situation, that which blocks our path actually presents a new path with a new part of us. If someone you love hurts you, there is a chance to practice forgiveness. If your business fails, now you can practice acceptance. If there is nothing else you can do for yourself, at least you can try to help others.

Problems, as Duke Ellington once said, are a chance for us to do our best.

Just our best, that's it. Not the impossible.

We must be willing to roll the dice and lose. Prepare, at the end of the day, for none of it to work.

Anyone in pursuit of a goal comes face-to-face with this time and time again. Sometimes, no amount of planning, no amount of thinking—no matter how hard we try or patiently we persist—will change the fact that some things just aren't going to work.

The world could use fewer martyrs.

We have it within us to be the type of people who try to get things done, try with everything we've got and, whatever verdict comes in, are ready to accept it instantly and move on to whatever is next.

Is that you? Because it can be.

PART III

Will

WHAT IS WILL? Will is our internal power, which can never be affected by the outside world. It is our final trump card. If action is what we do when we still have some agency over our situation, the will is what we depend on when agency has all but disappeared. Placed in some situation that seems unchangeable and undeniably negative, we can turn it into a learning experience, a humbling experience, a chance to provide comfort to others. That's will *power*. But that needs to be cultivated. We must prepare for adversity and turmoil, we must learn the art of acquiescence and practice cheerfulness even in dark times. Too often people think that will is how bad we want something. In actuality, the will has a lot more to do with surrender than with strength. Try "God *willing*" over "the will to win" or "*willing* it into existence," for even those attributes can be broken. True will is quiet humility, resilience, and flexibility; the other kind of will is weakness disguised by bluster and ambition. See which lasts longer under the hardest of obstacles.

THE DISCIPLINE OF THE WILL

Because he has become more myth than man, most people are unaware that Abraham Lincoln battled crippling depression his entire life. Known at the time as melancholy, his depression was often debilitating and profound—nearly driving him to suicide on two separate occasions.

His penchant for jokes and bawdy humor, which we find more pleasant to remember him for, was in many ways the opposite of what life must have seemed like to him during his darker moments. Though he could be light and joyous, Lincoln suffered periods of intense brooding, isolation, and pain. Inside, he struggled to manage a heavy burden that often felt impossible to lift.

Lincoln's life was defined by enduring and transcending great difficulty. Growing up in rural poverty, losing his mother while he was still a child, educating himself, teaching himself the law, losing the woman he loved as a young man, practicing law in a small country town, experiencing multiple defeats at the ballot box as he made his way through politics, and, of course, the bouts of depression, which at the time were not understood or appreciated as a medical condition. All of these were impediments that Lincoln reduced with a kind of prodding, gracious ambition, and smiling, tender endurance.

Lincoln's personal challenges had been so intense that he came to believe they were destined for him in some way, and that the depression, especially, was a unique experience that prepared him for greater things. He learned to endure all this, articulate it, and find benefit and meaning from it. Understanding this is key to understanding the man's greatness.

For most of Lincoln's political career, slavery was a dark cloud that hung over our entire nation, a cloud that portended an awful storm. Some ran from it, others resigned themselves to it or became apologists, most assumed it meant the permanent breakup of the Union—or worse, the end of the world as they knew it.

It came to be that every quality produced by Lincoln's personal journey was exactly what was required to lead the nation through its own journey and trial. Unlike other politicians, he was not tempted to lose himself in petty conflict and distractions, he could not be sanguine, he could not find it in his heart to hate like others would. His own experience with suffering drove his compassion to allay it in others. He was patient because he knew that difficult things took time. Above all, he found purpose and relief in a cause bigger than himself and his personal struggles.

The nation called for a leader of magnanimity and force of purpose—it found one in Lincoln, a political novice who was nevertheless a seasoned expert on matters of will and patience. These attributes were born of his own "severe experience," as he often called it, and the characteristics were representative of a singular ability to lead the nation through one of its most difficult and painful trials: the Civil War.

As crafty and ambitious and smart as he was, Lincoln's real strength was his will: the way he was able to resign himself to an onerous task without giving in to hopelessness, the way he could contain both humor and deadly seriousness, the way he could use his own private turmoil to teach and help others, the way he was able to rise above the din and see politics *philosophically*. "This too shall pass" was Lincoln's favorite saying, one he once said was applicable in any and every situation one could encounter.

To live with his depression, Lincoln had developed a strong inner fortress that girded him. And in 1861 it again gave him what he needed in order to endure and struggle through a war that was about to begin. Over four years, the war was to become nearly incomprehensibly violent, and Lincoln, who'd attempted at first to prevent it, would fight to win justly, and finally try to end it with "malice towards none." Admiral David Porter, who was with Lincoln in his last days, described it as though Lincoln "seemed to think only that he had an unpleasant duty to perform" and set himself to "perform it as smoothly as possible."

We should count ourselves lucky to never experience such a trial, or be required, as Lincoln had been, to hold and be able to draw from our personal woe in order to surmount it. But we certainly can and must learn from his poise and courage.

Clearheadedness and action are not always enough, in politics or in life. Some obstacles are beyond a snap of the fingers or novel solution. It is not always possible for one man to rid the world of a great evil or stop a country bent toward conflict. Of course, we try—because it *can* happen. But we should be ready for it not to. And we need to be able to find a greater purpose in this suffering and handle it with firmness and forbearance.

This was Lincoln: always ready with a new idea or innovative approach (whether it was sending a supply boat instead of reinforcements to the troops besieged at Fort Sumter, or timing the Emancipation Proclamation with a Union victory at Antietam to back it with the appearance of strength) but equally prepared for the worst. And then prepared to make the best of the worst.

Leadership requires determination and energy. And certain situations, at times, call on leaders to marshal that determined energy simply to endure. To provide strength in terrible times. Because of what Lincoln had gone through, because of what he'd struggled with and learned to cope with in his own life, he was able to lead. To hold a nation, a cause, an effort, together.

This is the avenue for the final discipline: the Will. If Perception and Action were the disciplines of the mind and the body, then Will is the discipline of the heart and the soul. The will is the one thing *we* control completely, always. Whereas I can *try* to mitigate harmful perceptions and give 100 percent of my energy to actions, those attempts can be thwarted or inhibited. My will is different, because it is within me.

Will is fortitude and wisdom—not just about specific obstacles but about life itself and where the obstacles we are facing fit within it. It gives us ultimate strength. As in: the strength to endure, contextualize, and derive meaning from the obstacles we cannot simply overcome (which, as it happens, is the way of flipping the unflippable).

Even in his own time, Lincoln's contemporaries marveled at the calmness, the gravity, and compassion of the man. Today, those qualities seem almost godlike—almost superhuman. His sense of what needed to be done set him apart. As though he were above or beyond the bitter divisions that weighed everyone else down. As though he were from another planet.

In a way, he was. Or at least he had traveled from somewhere very far away, somewhere deep inside himself, from where others hadn't. Schooled in suffering, to quote Virgil, Lincoln learned "to comfort those who suffer too." This, too, is part of the will—to think of others, to make the best of a terrible situation that we tried to prevent but could not, to deal with fate with cheerfulness and compassion.

Lincoln's words went to the people's hearts because they came from his, because he had access to a part of the human experience that many had walled themselves off from. His personal pain was an advantage.

Lincoln was strong and decisive as a leader. But he also embodied the Stoic maxim: *sustine et abstine.* Bear and forbear. Acknowledge the pain but trod onward in your task. Had the war gone on even longer, Lincoln would have lead his people through it. Had the Union lost the Civil War, he'd have known that he'd done everything he could in pursuit of victory. More important, if Lincoln had been defeated, he was prepared to bear whatever the resulting consequences with dignity and strength and courage. Providing an example for others, in victory or in defeat—whichever occurred.

With all our modern technology has come the conceited delusion that we control the world around us. We're convinced that we can now, finally, control the uncontrollable.

Of course that is not true. It's highly unlikely we will ever get rid of all the unpleasant and unpredictable parts of life. One needs only to look at history to see how random and vicious and awful the world can be. The incomprehensible happens all the time.

Certain things in life will cut you open like a knife. When that happens—at that exposing moment—the world gets a glimpse of what's truly inside you. So what will be revealed when you're sliced open by tension and pressure? Iron? Or air? Or *bullshit*?

As such, the will is the critical third discipline. We can think, act, and finally *adjust* to a world that is inherently unpredictable. The will is what prepares us for this, protects us against it, and allows us to thrive and be happy in spite of it. It is also the most difficult of all the disciplines. It's what allows us to stand undisturbed while others wilt and give in to disorder. Confident, calm, ready to work regardless of the conditions. *Willing* and able to continue, even during the unthinkable, even when our worst nightmares have come true.

It's much easier to control our perceptions and emotions than it is to give up our desire to control other people and events. It's easier to persist in our efforts and actions than to endure the uncomfortable or the painful. It's easier to think and act than it is to practice wisdom.

These lessons come harder but are, in the end, the most critical to wresting advantage from adversity. In every situation, we can

Always prepare ourselves for more difficult times.
Always accept what we're unable to change.
Always manage our expectations.
Always persevere.
Always learn to love our fate and what happens to us.
Always protect our inner self, retreat into ourselves.
Always submit to a greater, larger cause.
Always remind ourselves of our own mortality.

And, of course, prepare to start the cycle once more.

BUILD YOUR INNER CITADEL

If thy faint in the day of adversity, thy strength is small.

—PROVERBS 24:10

By age twelve, Theodore Roosevelt had spent almost every day of his short life struggling with horrible asthma. Despite his privileged birth, his life hung in a precarious balance—the attacks were an almost nightly near-death experience. Tall, gangly, and frail, the slightest exertion would upset the entire balance and leave him bedridden for weeks.

One day his father came into his room and delivered a message that would change the young boy's life: "Theodore, you have the mind but haven't got the body. I'm giving you the tools to make your body. It's going to be hard drudgery and I think you have the determination to go through with it."

You'd think that would be lost on a child, especially a fragile one born into great wealth and status. But according to Roosevelt's younger sister, who witnessed the conversation, it wasn't. His response, using what would become his trademark cheerful grit, was to look at his father and say with determination: *"I'll make my body."*

At the gym that his father built on the second-floor porch, young Roosevelt proceeded to work out feverishly every day for the next five years, slowly building muscle and strengthening his upper body against his weak lungs and for the future. By his early twenties the battle against asthma was essentially over, he'd worked—almost literally—that weakness out of his body.

That gym work prepared a physically weak but smart young boy for the uniquely challenging course on which the nation and the world were about to embark. It was the beginning of his preparation for and fulfillment of what he would call "the Strenuous Life."

And for Roosevelt, life threw a lot at him: He lost a wife and his mother in rapid succession, he faced powerful, entrenched political enemies who despised his progressive agenda, was dealt defeat in elections, the nation was embroiled in foreign wars, and he survived nearly fatal assassination attempts. But he was equipped for it all because of his early training and because he kept at it every single day.

Are you similarly prepared? Could you actually handle yourself if things suddenly got *worse*?

We take weakness for granted. We assume that the way we're born is the way we simply are, that our disadvantages are permanent. And then we atrophy from there.

That's not necessarily the best recipe for the difficulties of life.

Not everyone accepts their bad start in life. They remake their bodies and their lives with activities and exercise. They prepare themselves for the hard road. Do they hope they never have to walk it? Sure. But they are prepared for it in any case.

Are you?

Nobody is born with a steel backbone. We have to forge that ourselves.

We craft our spiritual strength through physical exercise, and our physical hardiness through mental practice (*mens sana in corpore sano*—sound mind in a strong body).

This approach goes back to the ancient philosophers. Every bit of the philosophy they developed was intended to reshape, prepare, and fortify them for the challenges to come. Many saw themselves as mental athletes—after all, the brain is a muscle like any other active tissue. It can be built up and toned through the right exercises. Over time, their muscle memory grew to the point that they could intuitively respond to every situation. Especially obstacles.

It is said of the Jews, deprived of a stable homeland for so long, their temples destroyed, and their communities in the Diaspora, that they were forced to rebuild not physically but within their minds. The temple became a metaphysical one, located independently in the mind of every believer. Each one—wherever they'd been dispersed around the world, whatever persecution or hardship they faced—could draw upon it for strength and security.

Consider the line from the Haggadah: "In every generation a person is obligated to view himself as if he were the one who went out of Egypt."

During Passover Seder, the menu is bitter herbs and unleavened bread—the "bread of affliction." Why? In some ways, this taps into the fortitude that sustained the community for generations. The ritual not only celebrates and honors Jewish traditions, but it prompts those partaking in the feast to visualize and possess the strength that has kept them going.

This is strikingly similar to what the Stoics called the Inner Citadel, that fortress inside of us that no external adversity can ever break down. An important caveat is that we are not born with such a structure; it must be built and actively reinforced. During the good times, we strengthen ourselves and our bodies so that during the difficult times, we can depend on it. We protect our inner fortress so it may protect us.

To Roosevelt, life was like an arena and he was a gladiator. In order to survive, he needed to be strong, resilient, fearless, ready for anything. And he was willing to risk great personal harm and expend massive amounts of energy to develop that hardiness.

You'll have far better luck toughening yourself up than you ever will trying to take the teeth out of a world that is—at best—indifferent to your existence. Whether we were born weak like Roosevelt or we are currently experiencing good times, we should always prepare for things to get tough. In our own way, in our own fight, we are all in the same position Roosevelt was in.

No one is born a gladiator. No one is born with an Inner Citadel. If we're going to succeed in achieving our goals despite the obstacles that may come, this strength in will must be built.

To be great at something takes practice. Obstacles and adversity are no different. Though it would be easier to sit back and enjoy a cushy modern life, the upside of preparation is that we're not disposed to lose all of it—least of all our heads—when someone or something suddenly messes with our plans.

It's almost a cliché at this point, but the observation that the way to strengthen an arch is to put weight on it—because it binds the stones together, and only with tension does it hold weight—is a great metaphor.

The path of least resistance is a terrible teacher. We can't afford to shy away from the things that intimidate us. We don't need to take our weaknesses for granted.

Are you okay being alone? Are you strong enough to go a few more rounds if it comes to that? Are you comfortable with challenges? Does uncertainty bother you? How does pressure feel?

Because these things *will* happen to you. No one knows when or how, but their appearance is certain. And life will demand an answer. You chose this for yourself, a life of doing things. Now you better be prepared for what it entails.

It's your armor plating. It doesn't make you invincible, but it helps prepare you for when fortune shifts . . . and it always does.

ANTICIPATION
(THINKING NEGATIVELY)

Offer a guarantee and disaster threatens.

—ANCIENT INSCRIPTION AT THE ORACLE OF DELPHI

A CEO calls her staff into the conference room on the eve of the launch of a major new initiative. They file in and take their seats around the table. She calls the meeting to attention and begins: "I have bad news. The project has failed spectacularly. Tell me what went wrong?"

What?! But we haven't even launched yet . . .

That's the point. The CEO is forcing an exercise in hindsight—in advance. She is using a technique designed by psychologist Gary Klein known as a *premortem.*

In a *post*mortem, doctors convene to examine the causes of a patient's unexpected death so they can learn and improve for the next time a similar circumstance arises. Outside of the medical world, we call this a number of things—a debriefing, an exit interview, a wrap-up meeting, a review—but whatever it's called, the idea is the same: We're examining the project in hindsight, after it happened.

A *pre*mortem is different. In it, we look to envision what could go wrong, what will go wrong, in advance, before we start. Far too many ambitious undertakings fail for prevent-able reasons. Far too many people don't have a backup plan because they refuse to consider that something might not go exactly as they wish.

Your plan and the way things turn out rarely resemble each other. What you think you deserve is also rarely what you'll get. Yet we constantly deny this fact and are repeatedly shocked by the events of the world as they unfold.

It's ridiculous. Stop setting yourself up for a fall.

No one has ever said this better than Mike Tyson, who, reflecting on the collapse of his fortune and fame, told a reporter, "If you're not humble, life will visit humbleness upon you."

If only more people had been thinking worst-case sce-nario at critical points in our lifetimes, the tech bubble, En-ron, 9/11, the invasion of Iraq, and the real estate bubble might have been avoidable. No one wanted to consider what could happen, and the result? Catastrophe.

Today, the premortem is increasingly popular in busi-ness circles, from start-ups to Fortune 500 companies and the *Harvard Business Review.* But like all great ideas, it is actually nothing new. The credit goes to the Stoics. They even had a better name: *premeditatio malorum* (premedita-tion of evils).

A writer like Seneca would begin by reviewing or rehears-ing his plans, say, to take a trip. And then he would go over, in his head (or in writing), the things that could go wrong or prevent it from happening: a storm could arise, the captain could fall ill, the ship could be attacked by pirates.

"Nothing happens to the wise man against his expecta-tion," he wrote to a friend. ". . . nor do all things turn out for him as he wished but as he reckoned—and above all he reckoned that something could block his plans."

Always prepared for disruption, always working that disruption into our plans. Fitted, as they say, for defeat or victory. And let's be honest, a pleasant surprise is a lot better than an unpleasant one.

What if . . .

Then I will . . .

What if . . .

Instead I'll just . . .

What if . . .

No problem, we can always . . .

And in the case where nothing could be done, the Stoics would use it as an important practice to do something the rest of us too often fail to do: manage expectations. Because sometimes the only answer to "What if . . ." is, *It will suck but we'll be okay.*

Your world is ruled by external factors. Promises aren't kept. You don't always get what is rightfully yours, even if you earned it. Not everything is as clean and straightforward as the games they play in business school. Be prepared for this.

You have to make concessions for the world around you. We are dependent on other people. Not everyone can be counted on like you can (though, let's be honest, we're all our own worst enemy sometimes). And that means people are going to make mistakes and screw up your plans—not always, but a lot of the time.

If this comes as a constant surprise each and every time it occurs, you're not only going to be miserable, you're going to have a much harder time accepting it and moving on to attempts number two, three, and four. The only guarantee, ever, is that *things will go wrong*. The only thing we can use to mitigate this is anticipation. Because the only variable we control completely is ourselves.

Common wisdom provides us with the maxims:

Beware the calm before the storm.
Hope for the best, prepare for the worst.
The worst is yet to come.
It gets worse before it gets better.

The world might call you a pessimist. Who cares? It's far better to seem like a downer than to be blindsided or caught off guard. It's better to meditate on what could happen, to probe for weaknesses in our plans, so those inevitable failures can be correctly perceived, appropriately addressed, or simply endured.

Then, the real reason we won't have any problem thinking about bad luck is because we're not afraid of what it portends. We're prepared in advance for adversity—it's other people who are not. In other words, this bad luck is actually a chance for us to make up some time. We're like runners who train on hills or at altitude so they can beat the runners who expected the course would be flat.

Anticipation doesn't magically make things easier, of course. But we are prepared for them to be as hard as they need to be, as hard as they actually are.

As a result of our anticipation, we understand the range of potential outcomes and know that they are not all good (they rarely are). We can accommodate ourselves to any of them. We understand that it could possibly all go wrong. And now we can get back to the task at hand.

You know you want to accomplish X, so you invest time, money, and relationships into achieving it. About the worst thing that can happen is not something going wrong, but something going wrong and catching you by surprise. Why? Because unexpected failure is discouraging and being beaten back hurts.

But the person who has rehearsed in their mind what could go wrong will not be caught by surprise. The person ready to be disappointed won't be. They will have the strength to bear it. They are not as likely to get discouraged or to shirk from the task that lies before them, or make a mistake in the face of it.

You know what's better than building things up in your imagination? Building things up in real life. Of course, it's a lot more fun to build things up in your imagination than it is to tear them down. But what purpose does that serve? It only sets you up for disappointment. Chimeras are like bandages—they hurt only when torn away.

With anticipation, we have time to raise defenses, or even avoid them entirely. We're ready to be driven off course because we've plotted a way back. We can resist going to pieces if things didn't go as planned. With anticipation, we can endure.

We are prepared for failure and ready for success.

THE ART OF ACQUIESCENCE

The Fates guide the person who accepts them and
hinder the person who resists them.

—CLEANTHES

Thomas Jefferson: born quiet, contemplative, and reserved—
purportedly with a speech impediment. Compared to
the great orators of his time—Patrick Henry, John Wesley,
Edmund Burke—he was a terrible public speaker.

His heart set on politics, he had two options: Fight against
this sentence, or accept it.

He chose the latter, channeling the energy into his writing, which others put into oratory instead. There he found
his medium. He found he could express himself clearly.
Writing was his strength. Jefferson was the one the founding
fathers turned to when they needed the Declaration of Independence. He wrote one of the most important documents
in history, in a single draft.

Jefferson just wasn't a public speaker—that doesn't make
him less of a man for acknowledging it and acting accordingly.

Same goes for Edison, who, as most people have no idea,
was almost completely deaf. Or Helen Keller, who was deaf
and blind. For both, it was the deprivation of these senses—

and acceptance rather than resentment of that fact—that allowed them to develop different, but acutely powerful, senses to adjust to their reality.

It doesn't always feel that way but constraints in life are a good thing. Especially if we can accept them and let them direct us. They push us to places and to develop skills that we'd otherwise never have pursued. Would we rather have everything? Sure, but that isn't up to us.

"True genius," as the infamous Dr. Samuel Johnson once said, "is a mind of large general powers accidentally determined in some particular direction."

That channeling requires consent. It requires acceptance. We have to allow some accidents to happen to us.

I can't just give up! I want to fight!

You know you're not the only one who has to accept things you don't necessarily like, right? It's part of the human condition.

If someone we knew took traffic signals personally, we would judge them insane.

Yet this is exactly what life is doing to us. It tells us to come to a stop here. Or that some intersection is blocked or that a particular road has been rerouted through an inconvenient detour. We can't argue or yell this problem away. We simply accept it.

That is not to say we allow it to prevent us from reaching our ultimate destination. But it does change the way we travel to get there and the duration of the trip.

When a doctor gives you orders or a diagnosis—even if it's the opposite of what you wanted—what do you do? You accept it. You don't have to like or enjoy the treatment but you know that denying it only delays the cure.

After you've distinguished between the things that are up to you and the things that aren't (*ta eph'hemin, ta ouk eph'hemin*), and the break comes down to something you don't control . . . you've got only one option: *acceptance.*

The shot didn't go in.

The stock went to zero.

The weather disrupted the shipment.

Say it with me: *C'est la vie. It's all fine.*

You don't have to like something to master it—or to use it to some advantage. When the cause of our problem lies outside of us, we are better for accepting it and moving on. For ceasing to kick and fight against it, and coming to terms with it. The Stoics have a beautiful name for this attitude. They call it the Art of Acquiescence.

Let's be clear, that is not the same thing as giving up. This has nothing to do with action—this is for the things that are immune to action. It is far easier to talk of the way things *should* be. It takes toughness, humility, and will to accept them for what they actually are. It takes a real man or woman to face *necessity.*

All external events can be equally beneficial to us because we can turn them all upside down and make use of them. They can teach us a lesson we were reluctant to otherwise learn.

For instance, in 2006 a long-term hip injury finally caught up with Lakers' coach Phil Jackson, and the surgery he had to fix it severely limited his courtside movement. Relegated to a special captain's-style chair near the players, he couldn't pace the sideline or interact with the team the same way. Initially, Jackson was worried this would affect his coaching. In fact, sitting back on the sideline above the rest of the bench *in-*

creased his authority. He learned how to assert himself without ever being overbearing the way he'd been in the past.

But to get these unexpected benefits we first have to accept the unexpected costs—even though we'd rather not have them in the first place.

Unfortunately, we are often too greedy to do this. We instinctively think about how much better we'd like any given situation to be. We start thinking about what we'd rather have. Rarely do we consider how much worse things could have been.

And things can *always* be worse. Not to be glib, but the next time you:

Lose money?
Remember, you could have lost a friend.
Lost that job?
What if you'd lost a limb?
Lost your house?
You could have lost *everything*.

Yet we squirm and complain about what was taken from us. We still can't appreciate what we have.

The hubris at the core of this notion that we can change everything is somewhat new. In a world where we can beam documents around the world in nanoseconds, chat in high-definition video with anyone anywhere, predict the weather down to the minute, it's very easy to internalize the assumption that nature has been domesticated and submits to our whim. Of course it hasn't.

People didn't always think this way. The ancients (and the not so ancients) used the word fate far more frequently than us because they were better acquainted with and exposed to how capricious and random the world could be. Events were considered to be the "will of the Gods." The Fates were forces that shaped our lives and destinies, often not with much consent.

Letters used to be signed "Deo volente"—God willing. Because who knew what would happen?

Think of George Washington, putting everything he had into the American Revolution, and then saying, "The event is in the hand of God." Or Eisenhower, writing to his wife on the eve of the Allied invasion at Sicily: "Everything we could think of have been done, the troops are fit everybody is doing his best. The answer is in the lap of the gods." These were not guys prone to settling or leaving the details up to other people—but they understood ultimately that what happened would happen. And they'd go from there.

It's time to be humble and flexible enough to acknowledge the same in our own lives. That there is always someone or something that could change the plan. And that person is not us. As the saying goes, "Man proposes but God disposes. "

As fate would have it.
Heaven forbid.
Nature permitting.
Murphy's Law.

Whatever version you prefer, it's all the same. Not that much has changed between their time and ours—they were just more cognizant of it.

Look: If we want to use the metaphor that life is a game,

it means playing the dice or the chips or the cards where they fall. Play it where it lies, a golfer would say.

The way life *is* gives you plenty to work with, plenty to leave your imprint on. Taking people and events as they are is quite enough material already. Follow where the events take you, like water rolling down a hill—it always gets to the bottom eventually, doesn't it?

Because (a) you're robust and resilient enough to handle whatever occurs, (b) you can't do anything about it anyway, and (c) you're looking at a big-enough picture and long-enough time line that whatever you have to accept is still only a negligible blip on the way to your goal.

We're indifferent and that's not a weakness.

As Francis Bacon once said, nature, in order to be commanded, must be obeyed.

LOVE EVERYTHING
THAT HAPPENS: *AMOR FATI*

> My formula for greatness in a human being is *amor fati*:
> that one wants nothing to be different, not forward,
> not backward, not in all eternity. Not merely bear what
> is necessary, still less conceal it . . . but love it.

—NIETZSCHE

At age sixty-seven, Thomas Edison returned home early
one evening from another day at the laboratory. Shortly
after dinner, a man came rushing into his house with urgent
news: A fire had broken out at Edison's research and produc-
tion campus a few miles away.

Fire engines from eight nearby towns rushed to the scene,
but they could not contain the blaze. Fueled by the strange
chemicals in the various buildings, green and yellow flames
shot up six and seven stories, threatening to destroy the entire empire Edison had spent his life building.

Edison calmly but quickly made his way to the fire,
through the now hundreds of onlookers and devastated em-
ployees, looking for his son. "Go get your mother and all her
friends," he told his son with childlike excitement. "They'll
never see a fire like this again."

What?!

Don't worry, Edison calmed him. "It's all right. We've just got rid of a lot of rubbish."

That's a pretty amazing reaction. But when you think about it, there really was no other response.

What should Edison have done? Wept? Gotten angry? Quit and gone home?

What, exactly, would that have accomplished?

You know the answer now: nothing. So he didn't waste time indulging himself. To do great things, we need to be able to endure tragedy and setbacks. We've got to love what we do and all that it entails, good and bad. We have to learn to find joy in every single thing that happens.

Of course, there was more than just a little "rubbish" in Edison's buildings. Years and years of priceless records, prototypes, and research were turned to ash. The buildings, which had been made of what was supposedly fire-proofed concrete, had been insured for only a fraction of their worth. Thinking they were immune to such disasters, Edison and his investors were covered for about a third of the damage.

Still, Edison wasn't heartbroken, not as he could have and probably should have been. Instead, it invigorated him. As he told a reporter the next day, he wasn't too old to make a fresh start. "I've been through a lot of things like this. It prevents a man from being afflicted with ennui."

Within about three weeks, the factory was partially back up and running. Within a month, its men were working two shifts a day churning out new products the world had never seen. Despite a loss of almost $1 million dollars (more than $23 million in today's dollars), Edison would marshal enough energy to make nearly $10 million dollars in revenue that year ($200-plus million today). He not only suffered a spectacular disaster, but he recovered and replied to it spectacularly.

The next step after we discard our expectations and *accept* what happens to us, after understanding that certain things—particularly bad things—are outside our control, is this: loving whatever happens to us and facing it with unfailing cheerfulness.

It is the act of turning what we *must* do into what we *get* to do.

We put our energies and emotions and exertions where they will have real impact. This is that place. We will tell ourselves: *This is what I've got to do or put up with? Well, I might as well be happy about it.*

Here's an image to consider: the great boxer Jack Johnson in his famous fifteen-round brawl with Jim Jeffries. Jeffries, the Great White Hope, called out of retirement like some deranged Cincinnatus to defeat the ascendant black champion. And Johnson, genuinely hated by his opponent and the crowd, still enjoying every minute of it. Smiling, joking, playing the whole fight.

Why not? There's no value in any other reaction. Should he hate them for hating him? Bitterness was their burden and Johnson refused to pick it up.

Not that he simply took the abuse. Instead, Johnson designed his fight plan around it. At every nasty remark from Jeffries's corner, he'd give his opponent another lacing. At every low trick or rush from Jeffries, Johnson would quip and beat it back—but never lose his cool. And when one well-placed blow opened a cut on Johnson's lip, he kept smiling—a gory, bloody, but nevertheless cheerful smile. Every round, he got happier, friendlier, as his opponent grew enraged and tired, eventually losing the will to fight.

In your worst moments, picture Johnson: always calm, always in control, genuinely loving the opportunity to prove himself, to perform for people, whether they wanted him to succeed or not. Each remark bringing the response it deserved and no more—letting the opponent dig his own grave. Until the fight ended with Jeffries on the floor and every doubt about Johnson silenced.

As Jack London, the famous novelist, reported from ringside seats:

> *No one understands him, this man who smiles. Well, the story of the fight is the story of a smile. If ever a man won by nothing more fatiguing than a smile, Johnson won today.*

That man is us—or rather, it *can* be us if we strive to become like him. For we're in our own fight with our own obstacles, and we can wear them down with our relentless smile (frustrating the people or impediments attempting to frustrate *us*). We can be Edison, our factory on fire, not bemoaning our fate but enjoying the spectacular scene. And then starting the recovery effort the very next day—roaring back soon enough.

Your obstacle may not be so serious or violent. But they are nevertheless significant and outside your control. They warrant only one response: a smile.

As the Stoics commanded themselves: Cheerfulness in all situations, especially the bad ones. Who knows where Edison and Johnson learned this epithet, but they clearly did.

Learning not to kick and scream about matters we can't control is one thing. Indifference and acceptance are certainly better than disappointment or rage. Very few understand or practice that art. But it is only a first step. Better than all of that is love for *all* that happens to us, for every situation.

The goal is:

Not: *I'm okay with this.*
Not: *I think I feel good about this.*
But: *I feel great about it.*
Because if it happened, then it was meant to happen, and I am glad that it did when it did. I am meant to make the best of it.

And proceed to do exactly that.

We don't get to choose what happens to us, but we can always choose how we feel about it. And why on earth would you *choose* to feel anything but good? We can choose to render a good account of ourselves. If the event must occur, *Amor fati* (a love of fate) is the response.

Don't waste a second looking back at your expectations. Face forward, and face it with a smug little grin.

It's important to look at Johnson and Edison because they weren't passive. They didn't simply roll over and tolerate adversity. They accepted what happened to them. They *liked* it.

It's a little unnatural, I know, to feel gratitude for things we never wanted to happen in the first place. But we know, at this point, the opportunities and benefits that lie within adversities. We know that in overcoming them, we emerge stronger, sharper, empowered. There is little reason to delay these feelings. To begrudgingly acknowledge later that it was for the best, when we could have felt that in advance because it was inevitable.

You love it because it's all fuel. And you don't just want fuel. You need it. You can't go anywhere without it. No one or no thing can. So you're grateful for it.

That is not to say that the good will always outweigh the bad. Or that it comes free and without cost. But there is always some good—even if only barely perceptible at first—contained within the bad.

And we can find it and be cheerful because of it.

PERSEVERANCE

"Gentleman, I am hardening on this enterprise. I repeat,
I am *now* hardening towards this enterprise."

—WINSTON CHURCHILL

Odysseus leaves Troy after ten long years of war destined for Ithaca, for home. If only he knew what was ahead of him: ten more years of travel. That he'd come so close to the shores of his homeland, his queen and young son, only to be blown back again.

That he'd face storms, temptation, a Cyclops, deadly whirlpools, and a six-headed monster. Or that he'd be held captive for seven years and suffer the wrath of Poseidon. And, of course, that back in Ithaca his rivals were circling, trying to take his kingdom and his wife.

How did he get through it? How did the hero make it home despite it all?

Creativity, of course. And craftiness and leadership and discipline and courage.

But above all: perseverance.

We talked about Ulysses S. Grant across the river from Vicksburg, searching for some way, any way, to get across and take it. That's *persistence.* That was Odysseus standing at the gates of Troy, trying everything before the success of the Trojan horse. Persistence. Everything directed at one problem, until it breaks.

But a ten-year voyage of trials and tribulations. Of disappointment and mistakes without giving in. Of checking your bearings each day and trying to inch a little closer to home— where you'll face a whole other host of problems once you arrive. Ironhearted and ready to endure whatever punishment the Gods decide you must, and to do it with courage and tenacity in order to make it back to Ithaca? That's more than persistence, that's *perseverance.*

If persistence is attempting to solve some difficult problem with dogged determination and hammering until the break occurs, then plenty of people can be said to be persistent. But perseverance is something larger. It's the long game. It's about what happens not just in round one but in round two and every round after—and then the fight after that and the fight after that, until the end.

The Germans have a word for it: *Sitzfleisch.* Staying power. Winning by sticking your ass to the seat and not leaving until after it's over.

Life is not about one obstacle, but *many.* What's required of us is not some shortsighted focus on a single facet of a problem, but simply a determination that we *will* get to where we need to go, somehow, someway, and nothing will stop us.

We will overcome every obstacle—and there will be many in life—until we get there. Persistence is an action. Perseverance is a matter of will. One is energy. The other, *endurance.*

And, of course, they work in conjunction with each other. That Tennyson line in full:

Made weak by time and fate, but strong in will
To strive, to seek, to find, and not to yield

Persist and persevere.

Throughout human history, there have been many strategies for overcoming the seemingly endless problems that affect us as individuals and as a group. Sometimes the solution was technology, sometimes it was violence, sometimes it was a radical new way of thinking that changed everything.

We've looked at a lot of those examples. But across the board, one strategy has been more effective than all the others, and it is responsible for far more than anything else. It works in good situations and in bad situations, dangerous situations and seemingly hopeless situations.

When Antonio Pigafetta, the assistant to Magellan on his trip around the world, reflected on his boss's greatest and most admirable skill, what do you think he said? It had nothing to do with sailing. The secret to his success, Pigafetta said, was Magellan's ability to endure hunger better than the other men.

There are far more failures in the world due to a collapse of will than there will ever be from objectively conclusive external events.

Perseverance. Force of purpose. Indomitable will. Those traits were once uniquely part of the American DNA. But they've been weakening for some time. As Emerson wrote in 1841,

If our young men miscarry in their first enterprises, they lose all heart. If the young merchant fails, men say he is ruined. If the finest genius studies at one of our colleges, and is not installed in an office within one year afterwards in the cities or suburbs of Boston or New York, it seems to his friends and to himself that he is right in being disheartened, and in complaining the rest of his life.

Think of what he'd say about us now. What would he say about you?

The majority of my generation decides to move back in with their parents after college. Unemployment, for them, is twice the national average. According to one 2011 study by the University of Michigan, many graduates aren't even bothering to learn how to drive. *The road is blocked,* they are saying, *so why get a license I won't be able to use?*

We whine and complain and mope when things won't go our way. We're crushed when what we were "promised" is revoked—as if that's not allowed to happen. Instead of doing much about it, we sit at home and play video games or travel or worse, pay for more school with more loan debt that will never be forgiven. And then we wonder why it isn't getting any better.

We'd be so much better following the lead of Emerson's counterexample. Someone who is willing to try not one thing, but "tries all the professions, who teams it, farms it, peddles, keeps a school, preaches, edits a newspaper, goes to Congress, buys a township, and so forth, in successive years, and always, like a cat, falls on his feet."

This is perseverance. And with it, Emerson said, "with the exercise of self-trust, new powers shall appear." The good thing about true perseverance is that it can't be stopped by anything besides death. To quote Beethoven: "The barriers are not erected which can say to aspiring talents and industry, Thus far and no farther."

We can go around or under or backward. We can decide that momentum and defeat are not mutually exclusive—we can keep going, advancing, even if we've been stopped in one particular direction.

Our actions can be constrained, but our will can't be. Our plans—even our bodies—can be broken. But belief in ourselves? No matter how many times we are thrown back, we alone retain the power to decide to go once more. Or to try another route. Or, at the very least, to accept this reality and decide upon a new aim.

Determination, if you think about it, is invincible. Nothing other than death can prevent us from following Churchill's old acronym: KBO. Keep Buggering On.

Despair? That's on you. No one else is to blame when you throw in the towel.

We don't control the barriers or the people who put them there. But we control ourselves—and that is sufficient.

The true threat to determination, then, is not what happens to us, but us ourselves. Why would you be your own worst enemy?

Hold on and hold steady.

SOMETHING BIGGER
THAN YOURSELF

A man's job is to make the world a better place to live in, so far as he is able—always remembering the results will be infinitesimal—and to attend to his own soul.

—LEROY PERCY

A United States Navy fighter pilot named James Stockdale was shot down in North Vietnam in 1965. As he drifted back down to earth after ejecting from his plane, he spent those few minutes contemplating what awaited him down below. Imprisonment? Certainly. Torture? Likely. Death? Possibly. Who knew how long it would all take, or if he'd ever see his family or home again.

But the second Stockdale hit the ground, that contemplation stopped. He wouldn't dare think about *himself*. See, he had a mission.

During the Korean War a decade earlier, individual self-preservation showed its ugly side. In the terrible, freezing prison camps of that war, it had very much become every American soldier for himself. Scared to death, the survival instincts of American prisoners of war kicked in so overwhelmingly that they ended up fighting and even killing one

THE OBSTACLE IS THE WAY

another simply to stay alive, rather than fighting against their captors to survive or escape.

Stockdale (then, a commander), aware that he would be the highest-ranking Navy POW the North Vietnamese had ever captured, knew he couldn't do anything about his fate. But as a commanding officer, he could provide leadership and support and direction to his fellow prisoners (who included future senator John McCain). He could change *that* situation and not let history repeat itself—this would be his cause, and he would help his men and lead them. Which is exactly what he proceeded to do for more than seven years; two of which were spent wearing leg irons in solitary confinement.

Stockdale didn't take his obligation as a commander lightly. He went so far as to attempt suicide at one point, not to end his suffering but to send a message to the guards. Other soldiers in the war effort had given their lives. He would not disgrace them or their sacrifice by allowing himself to be used as a tool against their common cause. He would rather hurt himself than contribute—even against his will—to hurting or undermining others. He proved himself formidable to whatever physical harm his captors threatened him with.

But he was human. And he understood that his men were, too. The first thing he did was throw out any idealistic notions about what happens to a soldier when asked to give up information under hours of torture. So he set up a network of support inside the camp, specifically to help soldiers who felt ashamed for having broken under the pressure. *We're in this together,* he told them. He gave them a watchword to remind them: U.S.—Unity over Self.

John McCain in his own cell nearby responded in essentially the same way and was able to endure indescribable torture for the same reasons. Hoping to stain the McCain family's prestigious military legacy and the United States, the Vietcong repeatedly offered McCain the opportunity to be released and return home. He wouldn't take it. He would not undermine the cause, despite self-interest. He stayed and was tortured—by choice.

These two men were not zealots for the cause—they certainly had their own doubts about the war in Vietnam. But their cause was their men. They cared about their fellow prisoners and drew great strength by putting their well-being ahead of their own.

Hopefully, you will not find yourself in a POW camp anytime soon. But we are in our own tough economic times—in fact, they can sometimes feel downright desperate.

You're young, you didn't cause this, it isn't your fault. We all got screwed. This only makes it easier to lose our sense of self, to say nothing of our sense of others. To think—if only privately—*I don't care about them, I've got to get mine before it's too late.*

Especially when the leaders in your supposed community make it clear that that is exactly how they feel about you when it comes down to the crunch. But no, ignore that. It is in this moment that we must show the true strength of will within us.

A few years ago, in the middle of the financial crisis, the artist and musician Henry Rollins managed to express this deeply human obligation better than millennia of religious doctrine ever have:

> *People are getting a little desperate. People might not show their best elements to you. You must never lower yourself to being a per-*

*son you don't like. There is no better time than now to have a moral
and civic backbone. To have a moral and civic true north. This is
a tremendous opportunity for you, a young person, to be heroic.*

Not that you need to martyr yourself. See, when we focus
on others, on helping them or simply providing a good example, our own personal fears and troubles will diminish.
With fear or heartache no longer our primary concern, we
don't have time for it. Shared purpose gives us strength.

The desire to quit or compromise on principles suddenly
feels rather selfish when we consider the people who would
be affected by that decision. When it comes to obstacles and
whatever reactions they provoke—boredom, hatred, frustration, or confusion—just because you feel that way, doesn't
mean everyone else does.

Sometimes when we are personally stuck with some in-
tractable or impossible problem, one of the best ways to create opportunities or new avenues for movement is to think:
*If I can't solve this for myself, how can I at least make this better for
other people?* Take it for granted, for a second, that there is
nothing else in it for us, nothing we can do for ourselves.
How can we use this situation to benefit *others?* How can we
salvage some good out of this? *If not for me, then for my family
or the others I'm leading or those who might later find themselves in
a similar situation.*

What doesn't help anyone is making this all about you, all
the time. *Why did this happen to me? What am I going to do about
this?*

You'll be shocked by how much of the hopelessness lifts
when we reach that conclusion. Because now we have something to *do.* Like Stockdale, now we have a mission. In the

light of blinding futility, we've got marching orders and things that must be done.

Stop making it harder on yourself by thinking about I, I, I. Stop putting that dangerous "I" in front of events. *I* did this. *I* was so smart. *I* had that. *I* deserve better than this. No wonder you take losses personally, no wonder you feel so alone. You've inflated your own role and importance.

Start thinking: *Unity over Self. We're in this together.*

Even if we can't carry the load all the way, we're going to take our crack at picking up the heavy end. We're going to be of service to others. Help ourselves by helping them. Becoming better because of it, drawing purpose from it.

Whatever you're going through, whatever is holding you down or standing in your way, can be turned into a source of strength—by thinking of people other than yourself. You won't have time to think of your own suffering because there are other people suffering and you're too focused on them.

Pride can be broken. Toughness has its limits. But a desire to help? No harshness, no deprivation, no toil should interfere with our empathy toward others. Compassion is always an option. Camaraderie as well. That's a power of the will that can never be taken away, only relinquished.

Stop pretending that what you're going through is somehow special or unfair. Whatever trouble you're having—no matter how difficult—is not some unique misfortune picked out especially for you. It just is what it is.

This kind of myopia is what convinces us, to our own detriment, that we're the center of the universe. When really, there is a world beyond our own personal experience filled with people who have dealt with worse. We're not special or unique simply by virtue of being. We're all, at varying points in our lives, the subject of random and often incomprehensible events.

Reminding ourselves of this is another way of being a bit more selfless.

You can always remember that a decade earlier, a century earlier, a millennium earlier, someone just like you stood right where you are and felt very similar things, struggling with the very same thoughts. They had no idea that you would exist, but you know that they did. And a century from now, someone will be in your exact same position, once more.

Embrace this power, this sense of being part of a larger whole. It is an exhilarating thought. Let it envelop you. We're all just humans, doing the best we can. We're all just trying to survive, and in the process, inch the world forward a little bit.

Help your fellow humans thrive and survive, contribute your little bit to the universe before it swallows you up, and be happy with that. Lend a hand to others. Be strong for them, and it will make you stronger.

MEDITATE ON YOUR MORTALITY

When a man knows he is to be hanged in a fortnight,
it concentrates his mind wonderfully.

—DR. JOHNSON

In late 1569, a French nobleman named Michel de Montaigne was given up as dead after being flung from a galloping horse.

As his friends carried his limp and bloodied body home, Montaigne watched life slip away from his physical self, not traumatically but almost flimsily, like some dancing spirit on the "tip of his lips." Only to have it return at the last possible second.

This sublime and unusual experience marked the moment Montaigne changed his life. Within a few years, he would be one of the most famous writers in Europe. After his accident, Montaigne went on to write volumes of popular essays, serve two terms as mayor, travel internationally as a dignitary, and serve as a confidante of the king.

It's a story as old as time. Man nearly dies, he takes stock, and emerges from the experience a completely different, and better, person.

And so it was for Montaigne. Coming so close to death energized him, made him curious. No longer was death something to be afraid of—looking it in the eyes had been a relief, even inspiring.

Death doesn't make life pointless, but rather purposeful. And, fortunately, we don't have to nearly die to tap into this energy.

In Montaigne's essays, we see proof of the fact that one can meditate on death—be well aware of our own mortality—without being morbid or a downer. In fact, his experience gave him a uniquely playful relationship with his existence and a sense of clarity and euphoria that he carried with him from that point forward. This is encouraging: It means that embracing the precariousness of our own existence can be exhilarating and empowering.

Our fear of death is a looming obstacle in our lives. It shapes our decisions, our outlook, and our actions.

But for Montaigne, for the rest of his life, he would dwell and meditate on that moment, re-creating the near-death moment as best he could. He studied death, discussing it, learning of its place in other cultures. For instance, Montaigne once wrote of an ancient drinking game in which participants took turns holding up a painting of a corpse inside a coffin and toasting to it: "Drink and be merry for when you're dead you will look like this."

As Shakespeare wrote in *The Tempest* not many years later, as he himself was growing older, "Every third thought shall be my grave."

Every culture has its own way of teaching the same lesson: *Memento mori,* the Romans would remind themselves. Remember you are mortal.

It seems weird to think that we'd forget this or need to be reminded of it, but clearly we do.

Part of the reason we have so much trouble with acceptance is because our relationship with our own existence is totally messed up. We may not say it, but deep down we act and behave like we're invincible. Like we're impervious to the trials and tribulations of morality. *That stuff happens to other people, not to ME. I have plenty of time left.*

We forget how light our grip on life really is.

Otherwise, we wouldn't spend so much time obsessing over trivialities, or trying to become famous, make more money than we could ever spend in our lifetime, or make plans far off in the future. All of these are negated by death. All these assumptions presume that death won't affect us, or at least, not when we don't want it to. The paths of glory, Thomas Gray wrote, lead but to the grave.

It doesn't matter who you are or how many things you have left to be done, somewhere there is someone who would kill you for a thousand dollars or for a vile of crack or for getting in their way. A car can hit you in an intersection and drive your teeth back into your skull. That's it. It will all be over. Today, tomorrow, someday soon.

It's a cliché question to ask, *What would I change about my life if the doctor told me I had cancer?* After our answer, we inevitably comfort ourselves with the same insidious lie: *Well, thank God I don't have cancer.*

But we do. The diagnosis is terminal for all of us. A death sentence has been decreed. Each second, probability is eating away at the chances that we'll be alive tomorrow; something is coming and you'll never be able to stop it. Be ready for when that day comes.

Remember the serenity prayer: If something is in our control, it's worth every ounce of our efforts and energy. Death is not one of those things—it is not in our control how long we will live or what will come and take us from life.

But thinking about and being aware of our mortality creates real perspective and urgency. It doesn't need to be depressing. Because it's invigorating.

And since this is true, we ought to make use of it. Instead of denying—or worse, fearing—our mortality, we can embrace it.

Reminding ourselves each day that we will die helps us treat our time as a gift. Someone on a deadline doesn't indulge himself with attempts at the impossible, he doesn't waste time complaining about how he'd like things to be.

They figure out what they need to do and do it, fitting in as much as possible before the clock expires. They figure out how, when that moment strikes, to say, *Of course, I would have liked to last a little longer, but I made a lot of out what I was already given so this works too.*

There's no question about it: Death is the most universal of our obstacles. It's the one we can do the least about. At the very best, we can hope to delay it—and even then, we'll still succumb eventually.

But that is not to say it is not without value to us while we are alive. In the shadow of death, prioritization is easier. As are graciousness and appreciation and principles. Everything falls in its proper place and perspective. Why would you do the wrong thing? Why feel fear? Why let yourself and others down? Life will be over soon enough; death chides us that we may as well do life right.

We can learn to adjust and come to terms with death—

this final and most humbling fact of life—and find relief in the understanding that there is nothing else nearly as hard left.

And so, if even our own mortality can have some benefit, how dare you say that you can't derive value from each and every other kind of obstacle you encounter?

PREPARE TO START AGAIN

Live on in your blessings, your destiny's been won.
But ours calls us on from one ordeal to the next.

—VIRGIL

The great law of nature is that it never stops. There is no end. Just when you think you've successfully navigated one obstacle, another emerges.

But that's what keeps life interesting. And as you're starting to see, that's what creates opportunities.

Life is a process of breaking through these impediments—a series of fortified lines that we must break through.

Each time, you'll learn something. Each time, you'll develop strength, wisdom, and perspective. Each time, a little more of the competition falls away. Until all that is left is you: the best version of you.

As the Haitian proverb puts it: Behind mountains are more mountains.

Elysium is a myth. One does not overcome an obstacle to enter the land of no obstacles.

On the contrary, the more you accomplish, the more things will stand in your way. There are always more obstacles, bigger challenges. You're always fighting uphill. Get used to it and train accordingly.

Knowing that life is a marathon and not a sprint is important. Conserve your energy. Understand that each battle is only one of many and that you can use it to make the next one easier. More important, you must keep them all in *real* perspective.

Passing one obstacle simply says you're worthy of more. The world seems to keep throwing them at you once it knows you can take it. Which is good, because we get better with every attempt.

Never rattled. Never frantic. Always hustling and acting with creativity. Never anything but deliberate. Never attempting to do the impossible—but everything up to that line.

Simply flipping the obstacles that life throws at you by improving in spite of them, *because* of them.

And therefore no longer afraid. But excited, cheerful, and eagerly anticipating the next round.

FINAL THOUGHTS

The Obstacle Becomes the Way

⚊⚊

Late in his reign, sick and possibly near death, Marcus Aurelius received surprising news. His old friend and most trusted general, Avidius Cassius, had rebelled in Syria. Having heard the emperor was vulnerable or possibly dead, the ambitious general had decided to declare himself Caesar and forcibly seize the throne.

Marcus should have been angry. History would have forgiven him for wanting to avenge this enemy. To crush this man who had betrayed him, who threatened his life, his family, and his legacy. Instead, Marcus did nothing—going as far as to keep the news secret from his troops, who might have been enraged or provoked on his behalf—but waited to see if Cassius would come to his senses.

The man did not. And so Marcus Aurelius called a council of his soldiers and made a rather extraordinary announcement. They would march against Cassius and obtain the "great prize of war and of victory." But of course, because it was Marcus, this war prize was something wholly different.

They would capture Cassius and endeavor not to kill him, but ". . . forgive a man who has wronged one, to remain a friend to one who has transgressed friendship, to continue faithful to one who has broken faith."

Marcus had controlled his perceptions. He wasn't angry, he didn't despise his enemy. He would not say an ill word against him. He would not take it personally. Then he acted—rightly and firmly—ordering troops to Rome to calm the panicking crowds and then set out to do what must be done: protect the empire, put down a threat.

As he told his men, if there was one profit they could derive from this awful situation that they had not wanted, it would be to "settle this affair well and show to all mankind that there is a right way to deal even with civil wars."

The obstacle becomes the way.

Of course, as so often happens, even the most well-intentioned plans can be interrupted by others. For both Cassius and Marcus, their destiny was changed when a lone assassin struck Cassius down in Egypt, three months later. His dream of empire ended right there. Marcus's initial hope to be able to forgive, in person, his betrayer ended as well.

But this itself created a better opportunity—the opportunity to practice forgiveness on a significantly larger scale. The Stoics liked to use the metaphor of fire. Writing in his journal, Marcus once reminded himself that "when the fire is strong, it soon appropriates to itself the matter which is heaped on it, and consumes it, and rises higher by means of this very material."

The unexpected death of his rival, the man whom Marcus had been deprived of granting clemency to, was this metaphor embodied. Marcus would now forgive essentially everyone involved. He wouldn't take any of it personally. He'd be a better person, a better leader for it.

Arriving in the provinces shortly after the death of Cassius, Marcus refused to put any coconspirators to death. He declined to prosecute any of the senators or governors who had endorsed or expressed support for the uprising. And when other senators insisted on death sentences for their peers associated with the rebellion, he wrote them simply: "I implore you, the senate, to keep my reign unstained by the blood of any senator. May it never happen."

The obstacle becomes the way, becomes the way.

Forever and ever and ever.

Yes, it's unlikely that anyone is going to make an armed run at our throne anytime soon. But people will make pointed remarks. They will cut us off in traffic. Our rivals will steal our business. We will be hurt. Forces will try to hold us back. Bad stuff will happen.

We can turn even this to our advantage. Always.

It is an opportunity. Always.

And if our only option—as was the case with Marcus— because of someone else's greed or lust for power, is simply to be a good person and practice forgiveness? Well, that's still a pretty good option.

This, I'm sure you've noticed, is the pattern in every one of the stories in this book.

Something stands in someone's way. They stare it down, they aren't intimidated. Leaning into their problem or weakness or issue, they give everything they have, mentally and physically. Even though they did not always overcome it in the way they intended or expected, each individual emerged better, stronger.

What stood in the way became the way. What impeded action in some way advanced it.

It's inspiring. It's moving. It's an art we need to bring to our own lives.

Not everyone looks at obstacles—often the same ones you and I face—and sees reason to despair. In fact, they see the opposite. They see a problem with a ready solution. They see a chance to test and improve themselves.

Nothing stands in their way. Rather, everything guides them on the way.

It is so much better to be this way, isn't it? There is a lightness and a flexibility to this approach that seem very different from how we—and most people—choose to live. With our disappointments and resentments and frustrations.

We can see the "bad" things that happen in our lives with gratitude and not with regret because we turn them from disaster to real benefit—from defeat to victory.

Fate doesn't have to be fatalistic. It can be destiny and freedom just as easily.

There is no special school that these individuals attended (aside from, for many, a familiarity with the ancient wisdom of Stoicism). Nothing that they do is out of reach for us. Rather, they have unlocked something that is very much within each and every person. Tested in the crucible of adversity and forged in the furnace of trial, they realized these latent powers—the powers of perception, action, and the will.

With this triad, they:

First, see clearly.
Next, act correctly.
Finally, endure and accept the world as it is.

Perceive things as they are, leave no option unexplored, then stand strong and transform whatever can't be changed. And they all feed into one another: Our actions give us the confidence to ignore or control our perceptions. We prove and support our will with our actions.

The philosopher and writer Nassim Nicholas Taleb defined a Stoic as someone who "transforms fear into prudence, pain into transformation, mistakes into initiation and desire into undertaking." It's a loop that becomes easier over time.

To be sure, no one is saying you've got to do it all at once. Margaret Thatcher didn't become known as the Iron Lady until she was sixty years old. There's a saying in Latin: *Vires acquirit eundo* (We gather strength as we go). That's how it works. That's our motto.

In mastering these three disciplines we have the tools to flip any obstacle upside down. We are worthy of any and every challenge.

Of course, it is not enough to simply read this or say it. We must practice these maxims, rolling them over and over in our minds and acting on them until they become muscle memory.

So that under pressure and trial we get better—become better people, leaders, and thinkers. Because those trials and pressures will inevitably come. And they won't ever stop coming.

But don't worry, you're prepared for this now, this life of obstacles and adversity. You know how to handle them, how to brush aside obstacles and even benefit from them. You understand the process.

You are schooled in the art of managing your perceptions and impressions. Like Rockefeller, you're cool under pressure, immune to insults and abuse. You see opportunity in the darkest of places.

You are able to direct your actions with energy and persistence. Like Demosthenes, you assume responsibility for yourself—teaching yourself, compensating for disadvantages, and pursuing your rightful calling and place in the world.

You are iron-spined and possess a great and powerful will. Like Lincoln, you realize that life is a trial. It will not be easy, but you are prepared to give it everything you have regardless, ready to endure, persevere, and inspire others.

The names of countless other practitioners escape us, but they dealt with the same problems and obstacles. This philosophy helped them navigate those successfully. They quietly overcame what life threw at them and, in fact, thrived because of it.

They were nothing special, nothing that we are not just as capable of being. What they did was simple (simple, not easy). But let's say it once again just to remind ourselves:

See things for what they are.
Do what we can.
Endure and bear what we must.

What blocked the path now is a path.
What once impeded action advances action.
The Obstacle is the Way.

POSTSCRIPT

You're Now a Philosopher. Congratulations.

⸺

To be a philosopher is not merely to have subtle thoughts,
nor even to found a school . . . it is to solve some of the
problems of life, not only theoretically, but practically.

—HENRY DAVID THOREAU

You now join the ranks of Marcus Aurelius, Cato, Seneca, Thomas Jefferson, James Stockdale, Epictetus, Theodore Roosevelt, George Washington, and many others.

All these men explicitly practiced and studied Stoicism—we know this for a fact. They were not academics, but men of action. Marcus Aurelius was emperor of the most powerful empire in the history of the world. Cato, the moral example for many philosophers, never wrote down a word but defended the Roman republic with Stoic bravery until his defiant death. Even Epictetus, the lecturer, had no cushy tenure—he was a former slave.

Frederick the Great was said to ride with the works of the Stoics in his saddlebags because they could, in his words, "sustain you in misfortune." Montaigne, the politician and essayist, had a line from Epictetus carved into the beam above the study in which he spent most of his time. George

Washington was introduced to Stoicism by his neighbors at age seventeen, then he put on a play about Cato to inspire his men in that dark winter at Valley Forge.

When Thomas Jefferson died, he had a copy of Seneca on his nightstand. The economist Adam Smith's theories on the interconnectedness of the world—capitalism—were significantly influenced by the Stoicism he'd studied as a schoolboy under a teacher who'd translated the works of Marcus Aurelius. Eugène Delacroix, the renowned French Romantic artist (known best for his painting *Liberty Leading the People*) was an ardent Stoic, referring to it as his "consoling religion." Toussaint Louverture, himself a former slave who challenged an emperor, read and was deeply influenced by the works of Epictetus. The political thinker John Stuart Mill wrote of Marcus Aurelius and Stoicism in his famous treatise *On Liberty*, calling it "the highest ethical product of the ancient mind."

The writer Ambrose Bierce, decorated Civil War veteran and contemporary of Mark Twain and H. L. Mencken, used to recommend Seneca, Marcus Aurelius, and Epictetus to aspiring writers who wrote to him, saying they'd teach them "how to be a worthy guest at the table of the gods." Theodore Roosevelt, after his presidency, spent eight months exploring (and nearly dying in) the unknown jungles of the Amazon, and of the eight books he brought on the journey, two were Marcus Aurelius's *Meditations* and Epictetus's *Enchiridion*.

Beatrice Webb, the English social reformer who invented the concept of collective bargaining, recalled the *Meditations* fondly in her memoirs as a "manual of devotion." The Percys, the famous Southern political, writing, and planting dynasty

(LeRoy Percy, United States senator; William Alexander Percy, *Lanterns on the Levee*; and Walker Percy, *The Moviegoer*) who saved thousands of lives during the flood of 1927, were well-known adherents to the works of the Stoics, because, as one of them wrote, "when all is lost, it stands fast."

In 1908, the banker, industrialist, and senator Robert Hale Ives Goddard donated an equestrian statue of Marcus Aurelius to Brown University. Eighty or so years after Goddard's donation, the Soviet poet, dissident, and political prisoner Joseph Brodsky wrote in his famous essay on the original version of that same statue of Marcus Aurelius in Rome that "if *Meditations* is antiquity, it is we who are the ruins." Like Brodsky, James Stockdale spent time imprisoned against his will—seven and a half years in a Vietcong prison camp, to be exact. And as he parachuted from his plane, Stockdale said to himself "I'm leaving the world of technology and entering the world of Epictetus."

Today, Bill Clinton rereads Marcus Aurelius every single year. Wen Jiabao, the former prime minister of China, claims that *Meditations* is one of two books he travels with and has read it more than one hundred times over the course of his life. Bestselling author and investor Tim Ferriss refers to Stoicism as his "operating system"—and, in the tradition of those who came before him, has successfully driven its adoption throughout Silicon Valley.

You might not see yourself as a "philosopher," but then again, neither did most of these men and women. By every definition that counts, however, they were. And now you are, too. You are a person of action. And the thread of Stoicism runs through your life just as it did through theirs—just as it has for all of history, sometimes explicitly, sometimes not.

The essence of philosophy is action—in making good on the ability to turn the obstacle upside down with our minds. Understanding our problems for what's within them and their greater context. To see things *philosophically* and *act* accordingly.

As I tried to show in this book, countless others have embodied the best practices of Stoicism and philosophy without even knowing it. These individuals weren't writers or lecturers, they were doers—like you.

Over the centuries though, this kind of wisdom has been taken from us, co-opted and deliberately obscured by selfish, sheltered academics. They deprived us of philosophy's true use: as an operating system for the difficulties and hardships of life.

Philosophy was never what happened in the classroom. It was a set of lessons from the battlefield of life.

The Latin translation for the title of *Enchiridion*—Epictetus's famous work—means "close at hand," or as some have said, "in your hands." That's what the philosophy was meant for: to be in your hands, to be an extension of you. Not something you read once and put up on a shelf. It was meant, as Marcus once wrote, to make us boxers instead of fencers—to wield our weaponry, we simply need to close our fists.

Hopefully, in some small way, this book has translated those lessons and armed you with them.

Now you are a philosopher and a person of action. And that is not a contradiction.

ACKNOWLEDGMENTS

It was Dr. Drew Pinsky, of all people, who introduced me to Stoicism. I was in college and I was invited to a small, private summit of college journalists that Dr. Drew, then the host of *Loveline,* was hosting. After it ended, he was standing in the corner and I cautiously made my way over to nervously ask if he had any book recommendations. He said he'd been studying a philosopher named Epictetus and that I should check it out.

I went back to my hotel room and ordered the book on Amazon along with another, *Meditations* by Marcus Aurelius. Marcus Aurelius, translated by Gregory Hays, arrived first. My life has not been the same since.

I want to thank Samantha, my girlfriend, whom I love more than anyone. We'd only been dating a few weeks, but I knew she was special when she went out and bought this book *Meditations,* the book I had been raving about. She deserves extra credit if only for enduring my many private and admittedly unstoic moments over the years. Thank you for coming on the many walks with me where I thought out loud. I want to thank my dog, Hanno—not that she is reading this—because she is a constant reminder of living in the present and of pure and honest joy.

The book you've just read would not have been possible without Nils Parker, whose editing and long talks shaped it. It would not exist without Stephen Hanselman, my agent who pushed for it, and my editor, Niki Papadopoulos, who believed in it and fought for what was a radical departure from my first book. Thanks to Adrian Zackheim for giving me my shot and providing a home for me as a writer at Portfolio.

I need to thank my master teacher and mentor Robert Greene, who not only subsidized my reading of many of the books I used as sources, but taught me the art of crafting a message and a book. His notes on my drafts were invaluable.

Thanks to Aaron Ray and Tucker Max, who showed me that a philosophic life and a life of action were not incompatible. Tucker, you're the one who encouraged me to read (and the one who told me to follow up Epictetus with Marcus Aurelius. I just found some endearing old e-mails where I asked you a million questions after I did). Thanks especially to Aaron, who pulled me out of school and forced me to live in the real world. Thanks to Tim Ferriss for encouraging me to write about Stoicism for his site back in 2009 and for our long talk in Amsterdam, which provided great additions to the book.

I owe Jimmy Soni and Rob Goodman for their excellent notes (and book on Cato), Shawn Coyne for his suggestion of a three-part structure, Brett Mckay of Art of Manliness .com for his book recommendations, and Matthias Meister for his insight and instruction in BJJ. Thanks to Garland Robinette, Amy Holiday, Brent Underwood, Michael Tunney, for their thoughts and feedback. Thanks to /r/stoicism on reddit, a great community who answered my questions and provoked many more. Thanks to New Stoa for their contributions to Stoicism online over the years.

In addition to the sources, I want to give profound thanks to the many other people and writers who exposed me to the stories and bits of wisdom in this book—I transferred much of it to my commonplace book and was so awed by the lessons that I didn't always record attribution. I very much see this book as a collection of the thoughts and actions of people better and smarter than me. I hope you read it the same way and attribute any credit deserved accordingly.

I must thank the National Arts Club, the Los Angeles Athletic Club, the New York Public Library, the libraries at the University of California, Riverside, and a bunch of different Starbucks and airplanes where I wrote or researched this book.

SELECTED BIBLIOGRAPHY

Alinsky, Saul. *Rules for Radicals.* New York: Vintage, 1989.

Aurelius, Marcus. *Meditations: A New Translation (Modern Library).* Translated by Gregory Hayes. New York: Modern Library, 2002.

Bakewell, Sarah. *How to Live: Or a Life of Montaigne in One Question and Twenty Attempts at an Answer.* New York: Other Press, 2010.

Becker, Gavin de. *The Gift of Fear and Other Survival Signals That Protect Us from Violence.* New York: Dell, 1999.

Bell, Madison Smartt. *Toussaint Louverture: A Biography.* New York: Pantheon, 2007.

Bonforte, John. *The Philosophy of Epictetus.* Literary Licensing, LLC, 2011.

Brodsky, Joseph. *On Grief and Reason: Essays.* New York: Farrar, Straus and Giroux, 1995.

Carroll, Paul B., and Chunka Mui. *Billion Dollar Lessons: What You Can Learn from the Most Inexcusable Business Failures of the Last 25 Years.* New York: Portfolio Trade, 2009.

Chernow, Ron. *Titan: The Life of John D. Rockefeller, Sr.* New York: Random House, 1998.

Cicero, Marcus Tullius. *On the Good Life (Penguin Classics).* Translated by Michael Grant. New York: Penguin, 1971.

Cohen, Herb. *You Can Negotiate Anything: The World's Best Negotiator Tells You How to Get What You Want.* New York: Bantam, 1982.

Cohen, Rich. *The Fish That Ate the Whale: The Life and Times of America's Banana King.* New York: Farrar, Straus and Giroux, 2012.

Critchley, Simon. *The Book of Dead Philosophers.* New York: Vintage, 2009.

Dio, Cassius. *The Roman History: The Reign of Augustus.* New York: Penguin, 1987.

Doyle, Charles Clay, Wolfgang Mieder, and Fred R. Shapiro. *The Dictionary of Modern Proverbs.* New Haven: Yale University Press, 2012.

Earhart, Amelia. *The Fun of It: Random Records of My Own Flying and of Women in Aviation.* Reprint edition. Chicago: Academy Chicago Publishers, 2000.

Emerson, Ralph Waldo. *Nature and Selected Essays.* New York: Penguin, 2003.

Epictetus. *Discourses and Selected Writings (Penguin Classics).* Translated by Robert Dobbin. New York: Penguin, 2008.

Epicurus. *The Essential Epicurus (Great Books in Philosophy).* Translated by Eugene O'Connor. Buffalo: Prometheus Books, 1993.

Evans, Jules. *Philosophy for Life and Other Dangerous Situations: Ancient Philosophy for Modern Problems.* Novato, CA: New World Library, 2013.

Everitt, Anthony. *The Rise of Rome: The Making of the World's Greatest Empire.* New York: Random House, 2012.

Feynman, Richard P. *Classic Feynman: All the Adventures of a Curious Character.* Edited by Ralph Leighton. New York: W. W. Norton, 2005.

Frankl, Viktor E. *Man's Search for Meaning.* New York: Touchstone, 1984.

Fraser, David. *Knight's Cross: A Life of Field Marshal Erwin Rommel*. New York: Harper Perennial, 1994.

Fronto, Marcus Cornelius. *Marcus Cornelius Fronto: Correspondence, I*. translated by C. R. Haines. Cambridge: Harvard University Press, 1919.

Goodman, Rob, and Jimmy Soni. *Rome's Last Citizen: The Life and Legacy of Cato, Mortal Enemy of Caesar*. New York: Thomas Dunne Books, 2012.

Graham-Dixon, Andrew. *Caravaggio: A Life Sacred and Profane*. New York: W. W. Norton, 2012.

Grant, Ulysses S. *Ulysses S. Grant: Memoirs and Selected Letters: Personal Memoirs of U. S. Grant/Selected Letters, 1839–1865*. New York: Library of America, 1990.

Greenblatt, Stephen. *Will in the World: How Shakespeare Became Shakespeare*. New York: Norton, 2005.

Greene, Robert. *The 48 Laws of Power*. New York: Viking Adult, 1998.

———. *33 Strategies of War*. New York: Penguin, 2007.

———. *Mastery*. New York: Viking Adult, 2012.

Greene, Robert, and 50 Cent. *The 50th Law*. New York: Harper, 2009.

Greitens, Eric. *The Heart and the Fist: The Education of a Humanitarian, the Making of a Navy SEAL*. New York: Houghton Mifflin Harcourt, 2011.

Hadot, Pierre. *The Inner Citadel: The Meditations of Marcus Aurelius*. Translated by Michael Chase. Cambridge: Harvard University Press, 2001.

———. *Philosophy as a Way of Life: Spiritual Exercises from Socrates to Foucault*. Translated by Arnold Davidson. Malden: Wiley-Blackwell, 1995.

———. *What Is Ancient Philosophy?* Translated by Michael Chase. Cambridge: Harvard University Press, 2004.

Haley, Alex. *The Autobiography of Malcolm X: As Told to Alex Haley*. New York: Ballantine Books, 1987.

Hart, B. H. Liddell. *Strategy*. New York: Penguin, 1991.

Heraclitus. *Fragments (Penguin Classics)*. Translated by Brooks Haxton. New York: Penguin, 2003.

Hirsch, James S. *Hurricane: The Miraculous Journey of Rubin Carter*. New York: Houghton Mifflin Harcourt, 2000.

Isaacson, Walter. *Steve Jobs*. New York: Simon & Schuster, 2011.

John, Tommy, with Dan Valenti. *TJ: My 26 Years in Baseball*. New York: Bantam, 1991.

Johnson, Jack. *My Life and Battles*. Edited and translated by Christopher Rivers. Washington, DC: Potomac Books, 2009.

Johnson, Paul. *Churchill*. New York: Viking, 2009.

———. *Napoleon: A Life*. New York: Viking, 2002.

Johnson, Samuel. *The Witticisms, Anecdotes, Jests, and Sayings, of Dr. Samuel Johnson, During the Whole Course of His Life*. Farmington Hills, MI: Gale ECCO Press, 2010.

Josephson, Matthew. *Edison: A Biography*. New York: Wiley, 1992.

Kershaw, Alex. *The Liberator: One World War II Soldier's 500-Day Odyssey from the Beaches of Sicily to the Gates of Dachau*. New York: Crown, 2012.

Lickerman, Alex. *The Undefeated Mind: On the Science of Constructing an Indestructible Self*. Deerfield Beach: HCI, 2012.

Lorimer, George Horace. *Old Gorgon Graham: More Letters from a Self-Made Merchant to His Son*. New York: Cosimo Classics, 2006.

McCain, John, and Mark Salter. *Faith of My Fathers: A Family Memoir*. New York: HarperCollins, 1999.

McPhee, John. *Levels of the Game*. New York: Farrar, Straus and Giroux, 1979.

———. *A Sense of Where You Are: Bill Bradley at Princeton*. New York: Farrar, Straus and Giroux, 1999.

Marden, Orison Swett. *An Iron Will*. Radford, VA: Wilder Publication, 2007.

————. *How They Succeeded: Life Stories of Successful Men Told by Themselves.* Hong Kong: Forgotten Books, 2012.

Meacham, Jon. *Thomas Jefferson: The Art of Power.* New York: Random House, 2012.

Millard, Candice. *The River of Doubt: Theodore Roosevelt's Darkest Journey.* New York: Doubleday, 2005.

————. *Destiny of the Republic: A Tale of Madness, Medicine and the Murder of a President.* New York: Doubleday, 2011.

Montaigne, Michel de. *The Essays: A Selection.* Translated by M. A. Screech. New York: Penguin, 1994.

Morris, Edmund. *The Rise of Theodore Roosevelt.* New York: Random House, 2010.

Musashi, Miyamoto. *The Book of Five Rings.* Translated by Thomas Cleary. Boston: Shambhala, 2005.

Oates, Whitney J. *The Stoic and Epicurean Philosophers: The Complete Extant Writings of Epicurus, Epictetus, Lucretius, Marcus Aurelius.* New York: Random House, 1940.

Paul, Jim, and Brandon Moynihan. *What I Learned Losing a Million Dollars.* New York: Columbia University Press, 2013.

Percy, William Alexander. *Lanterns on the Levee: Recollections of a Planter's Son.* Baton Rouge: LSU Press, 2006.

Plutarch. *The Makers of Rome: Nine Lives (Penguin Classics).* Translated by Ian Scott-Kilvert. New York: Penguin, 1965.

————. *On Sparta (Penguin Classics).* Translated and edited by Richard J. A. Talbert. New York: Penguin, 2005.

————. *Essays.* Edited by Ian Kidd. Translated by Robin H. Waterfield. New York: Penguin, 1993.

Pressfield, Stephen. *The War of Art: Winning the Inner Creative Battle.* New York: Rugged Land, 2002.

————. *Turning Pro: Tap Your Inner Power and Create Your Life's Work.* New York: Black Irish Entertainment, 2012.

————. *The Warrior Ethos.* New York: Black Irish Entertainment, 2011.

Ries, Eric. *The Lean Startup: How Today's Entrepreneurs Use Continuous Innovation to Create Radically Successful Businesses.* New York: Crown Business, 2011.

Roosevelt, Theodore. *Strenuous Epigrams of Theodore Roosevelt.* New York. HM Caldwell, 1904.

Sandlin, Lee. "Losing the War." *Chicago Reader.* March 6, 1997.

———. *Storm Kings: The Untold History of America's First Tornado Chasers.* New York: Pantheon, 2013.

Schopenhauer, Arthur. *Essays and Aphorisms (Penguin Classics).* Translated by R. J. Hollingdale. New York: Penguin, 1973.

———. *The Wisdom of Life and Counsels and Maxims.* Translated by T. Bailey Saunders. Buffalo: Prometheus Books, 1995.

Scott-Maxwell, Florida. *The Measure of My Days.* New York: Penguin, 1979.

Sellars, John. *Stoicism.* Berkeley: University of California Press, 2006.

Seneca, Lucius Annaeus. *Stoic Philosophy of Seneca: Essays and Letters.* Translated by Moses Hadas. New York: W. W. Norton, 1968.

———. *Letters from a Stoic (Penguin Classics).* Translated by Robin Campbell. New York: Penguin, 1969.

———. *On the Shortness of Life.* Translated by C.D.N. Costa. New York: Penguin, 2005.

Shenk, Joshua Wolf. *Lincoln's Melancholy: How Depression Challenged a President and Fueled His Greatness.* New York: Houghton Mifflin Harcourt, 2005.

Sherman, William Tecumseh. *Memoirs of General W. T. Sherman. (Library of America).* New York: Library of America, 1990.

Simpson, Brooks D. *Ulysses S. Grant: Triumph Over Adversity, 1822–1865.* New York: Houghton Mifflin Harcourt, 2000.

Smiles, Samuel. *Self-Help.* Berkeley: University of California Libraries, 2005.

Smith, Jean Edward. *Eisenhower in War and Peace*. New York: Random House, 2012.

Stockdale, James B. *Courage Under Fire: Testing Epictetus's Doctrines in a Laboratory of Human Behavior*. Stanford: Hoover Institution Press, 1993.

Taleb, Nassim Nicholas. *The Bed of Procrustes: Philosophical and Practical Aphorisms*. New York: Random House, 2010.

——. *Antifragile: Things That Gain from Disorder*. New York: Random House, 2012.

Taliaferro, John. *All the Great Prizes: The Life of John Hay, from Lincoln to Roosevelt*. New York: Simon & Schuster, 2013.

Vasari, Giorgio. *The Lives of the Most Excellent Painters, Sculptors, and Architects (Modern Library Classics)*. Edited by Philip Jack. Translated by Gaston du C. de Vere. New York: Modern Library, 2006.

Virgil, translated by Robert Fagles. *The Aeneid*. New York: Penguin, 2010.

Washington, George. *Washington on Courage: George Washington's Formula for Courageous Living*. New York: Skyhorse Publishing, 2012.

Watson, Paul Barron. *Marcus Aurelius Antoninus*. New York: Harper & Brothers, 1884.

Wilder, Laura Ingalls. *Writings to Young Women from Laura Ingalls Wilder—Volume Two: On Life as a Pioneer Woman*. Edited by Stephen W. Hines. Nashville: Tommy Nelson, 2006.

Wolfe, Tom. *A Man in Full*. New York: Farrar, Straus and Giroux, 1998.

——. *The Right Stuff*. New York: Picador, 2008.

Xenophon. *Xenophon's Cyrus the Great: The Arts of Leadership and War*. Edited by Larry Hedrick. New York: Truman Talley Books, 2006.

THE STOIC READING LIST

Stoicism is perhaps the only "philosophy" where the original, primary texts are actually cleaner and easier to read than anything academics have written afterward. Which is awesome because it means you can dive into the subject and go straight to the source. I firmly believe *everyone* is capable of reading these very accessible writers. Below are my recommendations both on specific translations and then some additional texts worth looking at.

***Meditations* by Marcus Aurelius (Modern Library).** There is *one* translation of Marcus Aurelius to read and that is Gregory Hayes's amazing edition for the Modern Library. Everything else falls sadly short. His version is completely devoid of any "thou's" "arts" "shalls." It's beautiful and hauting. I've recommended this book to literally thousands of people at this point. Buy it. Change your life.

***Letters of a Stoic* by Seneca** (see also: *On the Shortness of Life*). Both these translations by Penguin are fantastic. Seneca or Marcus are the best places to start if you're looking to explore Stoicism. Seneca seems like he would have been a fun guy to know—which is unusual for a Stoic. I suggest starting with *On the Shortness of Life* (a collection of short essays) and then move to his book of letters (which are really more like essays than true correspondence).

Discourses **by Epictetus (Penguin).** Personally, I prefer the Penguin translations, but I've tried a handful of others and found the differences to be relatively negligible. Of the big three, Epictetus is the most preachy and least fun to read. But he will also from time to time express something so clearly and profoundly that it will shake you to your core.

The above translations were the ones I used for this book.

OTHER BOOKS AND AUTHORS

I know this will seem harsh, but I strongly advise steering clear of most of the other books *about* Stoicism (and I've read them) with one exception: the works of Pierre Hadot. While all the other academics and popularizers of Stoicism mostly miss the point or needlessly complicate things, Hadot clarifies. His interpretation of Marcus Aurelius in the book *The Inner Citadel*—that Marcus was not writing some systemic explanation of the universe but creating a set of practical exercises the emperor was actually practicing himself—was a huge leap forward. His book *Philosophy as a Way of Life* explains how philosophy has been wrongly interpreted as a thing people *talk* about rather than something that people *do*. If you really want to dive into practical philosophy, Hadot is the guy to read. (Also his translations of Seneca, Marcus Aurelius, and Epictetus—which he does for himself from the originals in his analysis—are quite good.)

Some other great authors/philosophers to read—particularly their books of maxims or aphorisms, which are in line with a lot of stoic thinking:

Heraclitus
Plutarch
Socrates
Cicero
Montaigne
Arthur Schopenhauer

Penguin Random House published this book, but even if it hadn't, I would recommend starting with the Penguin Classics.

STOIC ARTICLES & ONLINE RESOURCES:

http://www.fourhourworkweek.com/blog/2009/04/13/
    stoicism-101-a-practical-guide-for-entrepreneurs/.
http://www.fourhourworkweek.com/blog/2012/10/09/
    stoicism-for-modern-stresses-5-lessons-from-cato/.
http://www.fourhourworkweek.com/blog/2011/05/18/
    philosophy-as-a-personal-operating-system-from-seneca-
    to-musashi/.
http://www.newstoa.com/ (the online stoic registry).
http://www.reddit.com/r/Stoicism (stoicism board on
    Reddit).

http://www.youtube.com/watch?v=nLD09Qa3kMk (an amazing lecture on stoicism).

http://philosophy-of-cbt.com/ (perhaps the best blog about stoicism out there).

http://philosophyforlife.org/ (the blog of prominent stoicism author Jules Evans).

READING RECOMMENDATIONS

This book and its stories were a result of the books I've been fortunate enough to come across in my life. Each month I distill what I read into a short e-mail of book recommendations, which I send to my network of friends and connections. The list started as about forty people and is now received and read by 10,000 people from all over the world. All in all, I've recommended, discussed and chatted more than a thousand books with these fellow readers in the last five years.

If you'd like to join us and get these recommendations, sign up at Ryanholiday.net/Reading-Newsletter/.

Or you can just send me an e-mail at ryan.holiday@gmail.com and tell me you want to get the e-mail (just put Reading List in the subject line).